Discovering JOY

NOT BECAUSE LIFE IS PERFECT,
BUT BECAUSE *God* IS FAITHFUL

Discovering Joy: Not Because Life is Perfect, but Because God is Faithful

Publisher:
Time-Warp Wife Ministries
114 Wyndham Estate Drive Steinbach, Manitoba
R5G 2K6

Interior design by Darlene Schacht
Cover design by Darlene Schacht
Some images from Adobe Stock Photo
Some images created using AI tools

ISBN 978-1-988984-29-2

Discovering JOY

NOT BECAUSE LIFE IS PERFECT, BUT BECAUSE *God* IS FAITHFUL

DARLENE SCHACHT

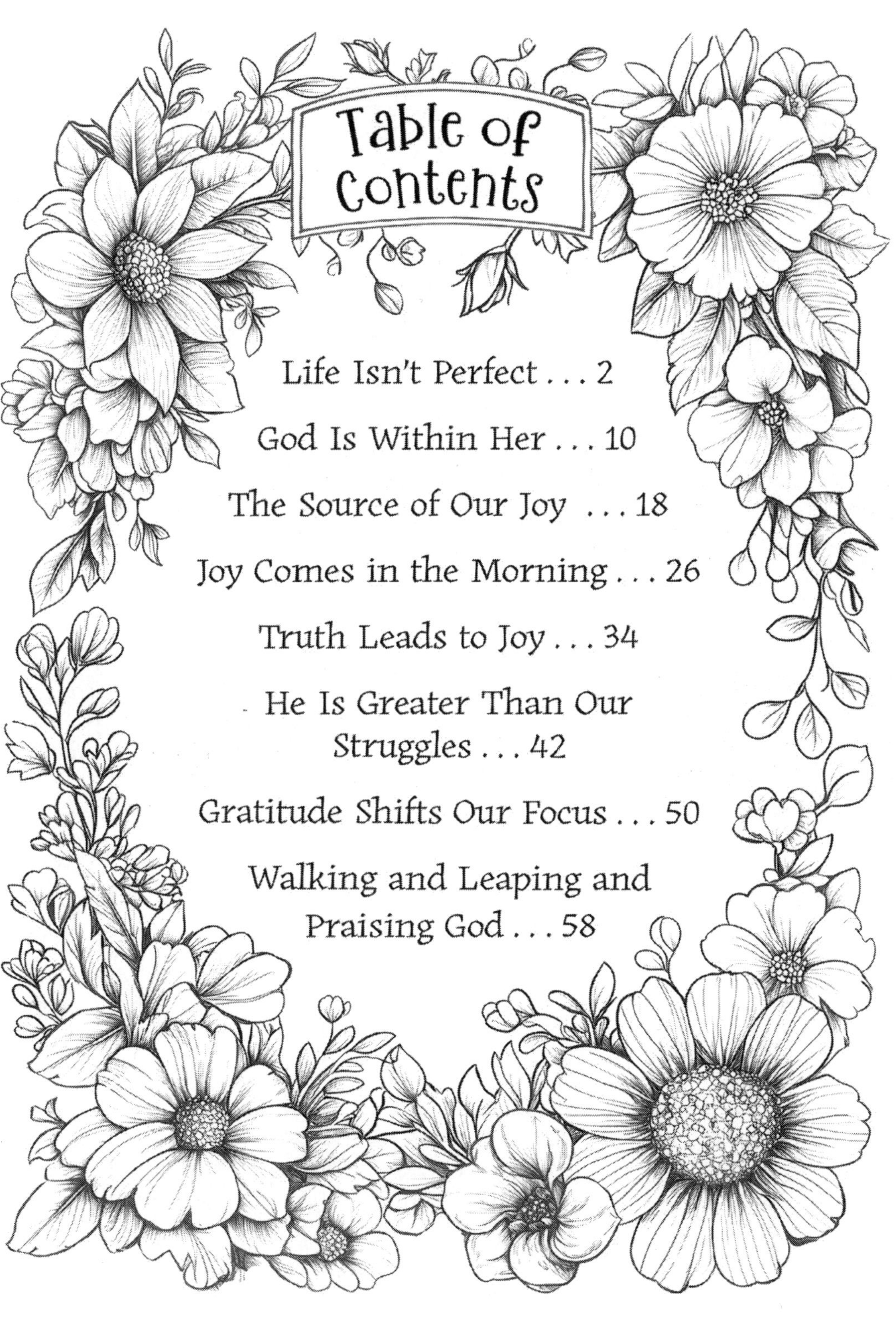

Table of Contents

Table of Contents Cont'd

Dear Friend,

Life isn't perfect. In fact, some days it's unsettling, unpredictable, and full of unexpected turns. And yet, in the middle of it all, there's joy. Not the fleeting kind that shifts with the winds of change, but a steadfast joy rooted in the faithfulness of God and held steady by His unchanging love.

This devotional was born out of life's imperfect moments. In fact, just before I started writing this book, I lost my oldest sister and our family dog—all in one heartbreaking week. It was a season that felt heavy with grief and uncertainty. And it wasn't the first storm I've weathered. I've walked through losses that shook my heart, including five miscarriages. I've faced personal failures that left me broken and in need of God's grace. I've experienced the wounds of an unhealthy relationship and carried the scars of those difficult years. But through every season, God has been my comfort and strength. I don't share these things lightly. I share them because I want you to know that I understand what it's like to feel lost, weary, and in need of hope.

But through it all, I've learned something beautiful: joy isn't about waiting for life to get easier. It's about discovering God's unshakable presence, right in the thick of it all. He meets us in our brokenness, gives us beauty for ashes, and offers a joy that the world can't take away.

Throughout these pages, I invite you to join me on a journey of renewal. Each chapter offers a short

devotional to encourage your heart, a reading prompt to guide your study, and verse maps—a unique way to help you dig deeper into Scripture. You'll also find moments of gratitude, practical ways to cultivate joy, and inspiring stories that remind us of God's goodness.

I know. If you're anything like me, you probably have a stack of devotionals lining your bookshelves right now. But this one is more than merely a book—it's an invitation to slow down, engage deeply with God's Word, and welcome His joy into your life.

My prayer for your journey is this: that you'll encounter the One who brings joy, and allow His presence to shape you. That you'll find peace in the One who sees your tears, hears your prayers, and feels your pain.

Whether you're in a season of rejoicing or a season of weeping, know this: joy is coming. God's promises are true, and His love for you is unwavering. Let this time of reflection fill you with joy as you draw closer to Him—because life isn't perfect, but we know God is faithful.

With love and joy,

Darlene Schacht
The Time-Warp Wife

Discover Other Studies by Darlene Schacht

These are just a few of my studies! I've written over 15 Bible studies to help women grow in faith and deepen their walk with God. You can find them all on Amazon or listed on my blog at **TimeWarpWife.com**.

Living Faithfully — Bible Study
A Journey Through James

Author Darlene Schacht guides you through the teachings of James, offering practical insights that resonate with everyday challenges. From understanding the importance of perseverance during trials to learning the power of words and the necessity of living a life that mirrors your faith, this study provides the tools you need to grow closer to God and live faithfully in every area of your life.

Jacob Bible Study: Pursuing God with Steadfast Faith & Unyielding Courage

Each chapter offers a unique perspective on Jacob's encounters with God, making this ancient story resonate with contemporary relevance and personal reflection. Perfect for both individual study and small groups, this book is designed to deepen your faith and enhance your understanding of Scripture.

The 7 Virtues of a Proverbs 31 Woman

Discover the timeless wisdom and transformative power of *The Proverbs 31 Woman* with this inspiring and practical Bible study. *The 7 Virtues of a Proverbs 31 Woman* dives deep into Scripture to help you understand and embody the essential qualities of a godly woman.

Perfect for individual study or group settings, this transformative resource is a must-have for women seeking to cultivate a life of grace, wisdom, and godly virtue.

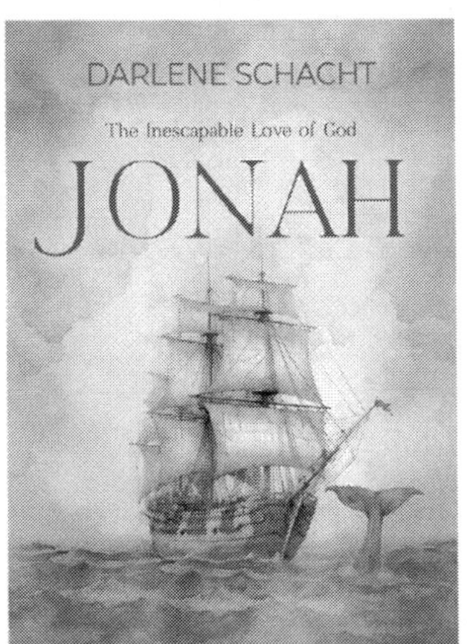

Jonah: The Inescapable Love of God

Journey through the compelling story of Jonah and experience firsthand the relentless love of God—love that pursues us, surrounds us, and ultimately transforms us. This enriching Bible study not only dives into the depths of God's compassion, it also explores our own human struggles with grace and purpose.

Ruth Bible Study: Echoes of Christ, Our Kinsman Redeemer

Embark on a profound journey through the Book of Ruth with New York Times best-selling author Darlene Schacht. This insightful guide illuminates the remarkable parallels of love and redemption that span thousands of years, highlighting how Christ is foreshadowed as our ultimate Kinsman Redeemer—a truth particularly evident in the developing relationship between Boaz and Ruth.

Though the fig tree does not bud
and there are no grapes
on the vines, though
the olive crop fails
and the fields
produce no food,
though there are
no sheep in the
pen and no
cattle in the
stalls, yet I will
rejoice in the LORD, I will
be joyful in God my
Savior. - Habakkuk 3:17-18

1 LIFE ISN'T PERFECT

Life isn't perfect. We've all been there—those days when it feels like everything is falling apart, and you're just trying to keep your head above water. For me, the last few months took a detour I wasn't prepared for. Not long after our Jeep was stolen, we lost our sweet bull mastiff and then my oldest sister passed away. While I was fighting the flu, I also had deadlines to meet for our upcoming Bible study.

> *"For I know the plans I have for you," declares the Lord, "plans to prosper you and not to harm you, plans to give you hope and a future."*
>
> —Jeremiah 29:11

I'm not sharing this to complain—not about the deadlines, anyway. Honestly, I'm so grateful for them. While the world around me began to unravel, God's Word was my lifeline. I'm convinced that being knee-deep in Scripture was exactly where I needed to be. In the shifting sands of grief and uncertainty, I was held firm by the certainty of His Word.

I feel the sting of losing a loved one, and yet there's a joy that coexists with my tears—not because life is perfect, but because God is faithful. I know that He's with me, and even in the darkest moments, I still find Him there. When everything else is uncertain, I can lean on His unshakable strength, trust in His unfailing Word, and stand on His unchanging promises.

Jeremiah 29:11 is a balm for the weary soul: "For I know the plans I have for you," declares the Lord, "plans to prosper you and not to harm you, plans to give you hope and a future." It's a verse many of us turn to when life feels unpredictable, as we cling to the promise of hope. But here's what I've been learning lately: the hope God gives us isn't tied to the outcome of our circumstances. It's rooted in the unchanging nature of who He is.

The context of this verse is so important. God spoke these words to His people while they were in exile, far from the comforts of home, immersed in uncertainty. This wasn't a quick fix or a promise of an easy life. It was God's reminder that even in their hardest seasons, He was working out His good plan. He saw their tears and struggles, but He also saw the restoration that was coming.

And isn't that true for us, too? God sees our broken places. He's not distant or detached. He's right here, working within us and around us, renewing our spirits and drawing us closer to Him. Even when we can't understand what He's doing, we can trust that He is faithful. And when we catch glimpses of His purpose, even in the smallest ways, we're reminded of His goodness.

So, if today feels heavy—if disappointment or loss has been weighing on your heart—let Jeremiah 29:11 remind you of this truth: God is designing your future. You're not forgotten. His promises are steadfast. Lean into His presence. Rest in His plan. And let Him do what only He can—renew your spirit and fill you with joy.

WORDS TO GROW BY

When life feels heavy and the burdens pile high, go to Him. Let His unchanging presence steady you. He sees your pain, your struggles, and your tears. But He also sees the restoration He is bringing. Trust in His plan, even when you don't understand it. Rest in His unshakable love, for He is your refuge. Cling to His Word and let it fill you with peace and joy that the world cannot give. With Him, you can walk through the uncertainty. Lean into His strength—He will never leave you nor forsake you.

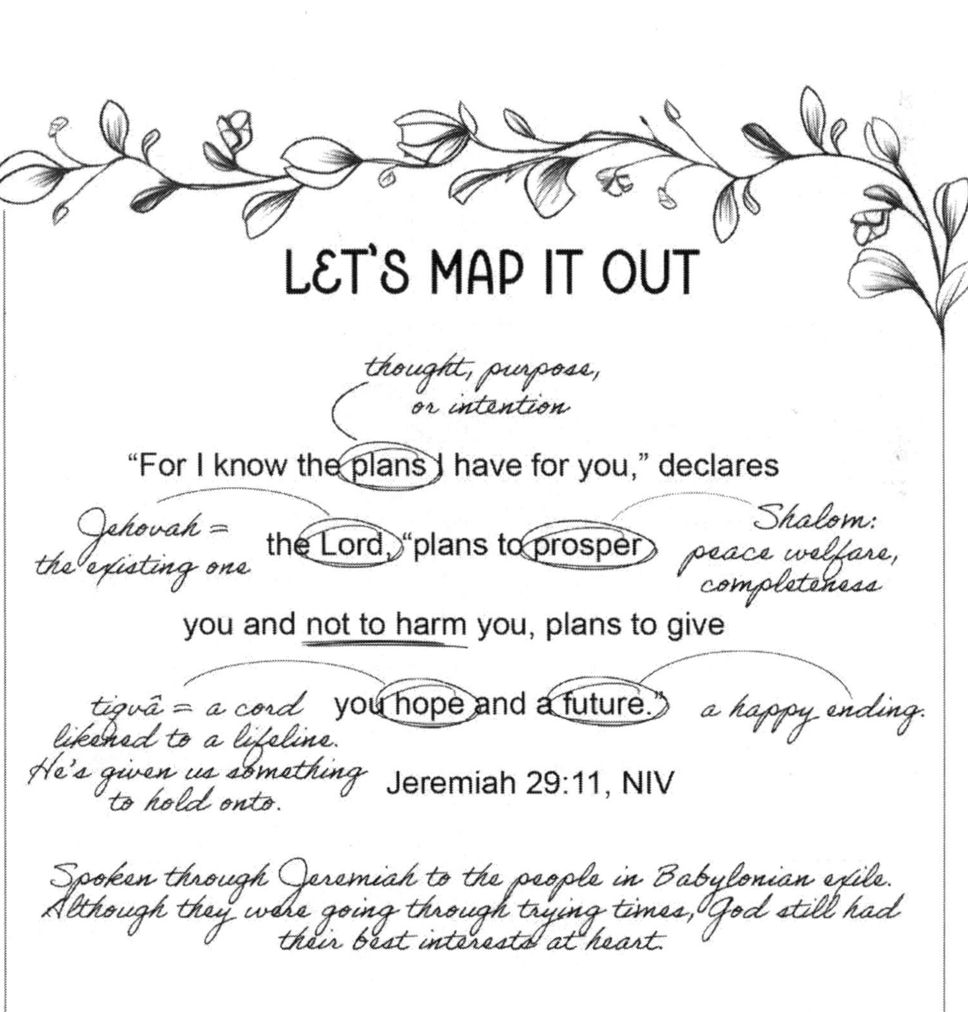

READ AND REFLECT

Read Jeremiah 29:4-14. How does God's faithfulness to the Israelites during their exile encourage you to trust Him in difficult times?

JOY IN THE SIMPLE THINGS

Use the space below to list four things that have brought you joy this past week:

1. ______
2. ______
3. ______
4. ______

GOD'S PERFECT PLAN

Jeremiah 29:11 reminds us that God is always at work, even when we can't see the full picture. His plans are good, His promises are sure, and His timing is perfect. More than just "beautiful words" the verse is a declaration that steadies the soul and fills us with joy. Here are five key takeaways to hold onto as we trust in His faithfulness:

GOD HAS A PLAN

- Even when life feels chaotic or uncertain, we can rest in the truth that God's plan is intentional and purposeful.

GOD'S PLANS BRING HOPE

- Trusting in Him gives us strength to face today and confidence for tomorrow.

GOD'S PLANS ARE GOOD

- No matter how difficult our journey might be, He has our best interest at heart.

GOD'S TIMING IS PERFECT

- God's plans unfold according to His perfect timing, even when we don't understand it.

GOD'S PROMISES BRING COMFORT

- In seasons of uncertainty, we can cling to this promise: God's plans will lead us to hope and a future. He is our refuge and strength.

More Food for Thought...

You turned my wailing into dancing; You removed my sackcloth and clothed me with joy.
–Psalm 30:11

Instead of your shame you will receive a double portion, and instead of disgrace you will rejoice in your inheritance. And so you will inherit a double portion in your land, and everlasting joy will be yours.
–Isaiah 61:7

May the God of hope fill you with all joy and peace as you trust in Him, so that you may overflow with hope by the power of the Holy Spirit.
–Romans 15:13

When anxiety was great within me, Your consolation brought me joy.
–Psalm 94:19

Rejoice greatly, Daughter Zion! Shout, Daughter Jerusalem! See, your king comes to you, righteous and victorious, lowly and riding on a donkey.
– Zechariah 9:9

Thoughts
and Jots

2

GOD IS WITHIN HER

> *God is within her,*
> *she will not fall;*
> *God will help her*
> *at break of day.*
>
> —Psalm 46:5

It was the spring of '78. Night Fever was climbing the charts, Grease made its debut in theaters, and my sister Bonnie and I were making ours in our junior high school's production of Oliver. After months of practicing lines, singing songs, and surviving dress rehearsals, the big night finally came. And let me just say—fear doesn't even begin to describe what we were feeling that night. Bonnie had the starring role, and I could see her nerves written all over her face as we waited backstage. My heart was pounding too. What if we forgot our lines? What if something embarrassing happened? We'd be sure to hear about it in class the next day.

All that changed the moment we stepped onto the stage and spotted our family. To our surprise, they'd bought out the entire front row! Those nine familiar faces were just the comfort we needed to get through the night. Suddenly, I wasn't worried about failing, slipping up, or forgetting my lines. I was held—completely safe in the warmth of their love. That feeling of safety brought with it a sense of joy I'll never forget.

Psalm 46:5 tells us, "God is within her, she will not fall; God will help her at break of day." That kind of reassurance transforms the way we face challenges, doesn't it? The presence of God is the steadying force that keeps us grounded. Like the moment I stepped into the spotlight and felt the support of my family strengthening me, God gives us the courage and strength to step out in faith.

Psalm 46 begins with these words: "God is our refuge and strength, an ever-present help in trouble." It's a reminder to us that life isn't easy, but our God is faithful. When everything feels uncertain, when fear or doubt creeps in, we have a pillar of strength to lean on. His faithfulness isn't dependent on us having it all together. It isn't diminished by life's imperfections. He is faithful because that's who He is. When we embrace this truth, it changes everything. Fear gives way to faith. Anxiety is replaced with peace. And joy? Joy becomes our constant companion.

Sometimes we get so focused on the chaos around us that we forget to look up. But when we shift our gaze to the One who holds us steady, everything changes. Joy becomes possible—not because circumstances improve, but because we remember He's there. And when God is with us, joy isn't fleeting; it's steadfast and sure.

Maybe you're in a season that feels overwhelming. Maybe you're backstage, so to speak, wondering if you might fail or fall. Can I remind you of something, my friend? God is already in the front row. His eyes are on you, and He's cheering you on. His presence will comfort and strengthen you, and His joy will sustain you.

PRACTICALLY SPEAKING

Today, look for one small way to embrace joy, even in the middle of a busy or challenging moment. It could be pausing to thank God for His presence, savoring a quiet moment with a cup of tea, sharing a smile with someone, or writing down three things you're grateful for. Let the reminder that "God is within her, she will not fall" bring you peace and gladness throughout your day.

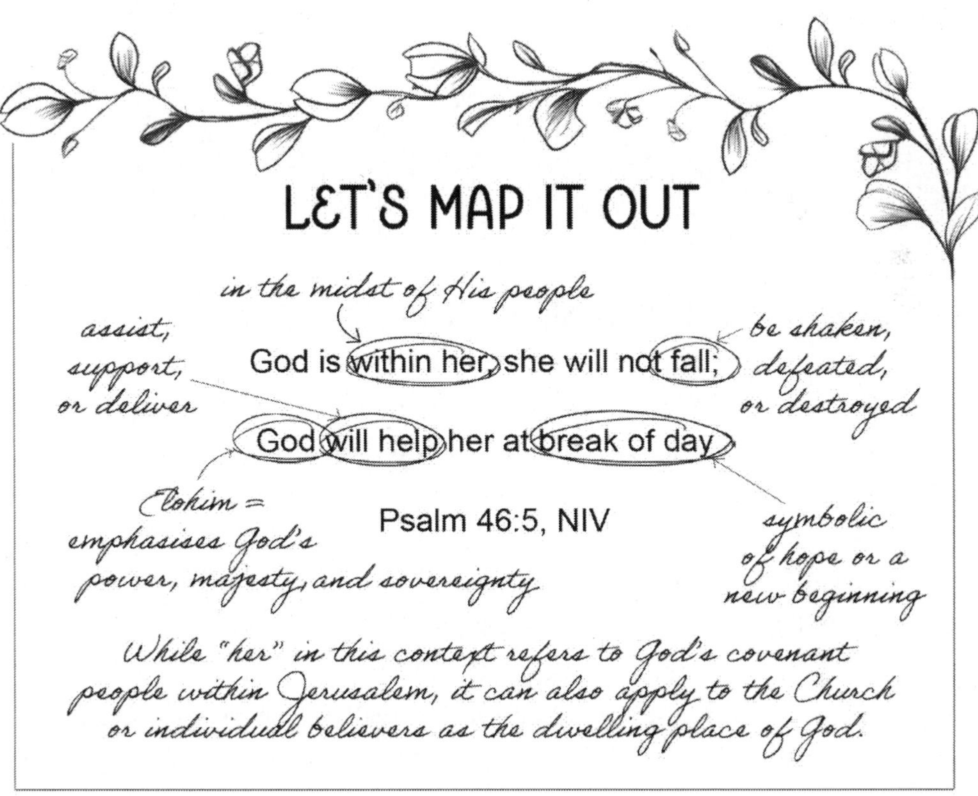

READ AND REFLECT

Read Psalm 46:1-7. What is it about the river in verse 4 that brings joy, and how does this contrast with the turbulent waters described in verses 2&3?

HOW GOD'S PRESENCE BRINGS JOY

God's presence shifts our perspective, lifting our burdens and reminding us that we are never alone. We find an example of this in 2 Kings 6:15-17. When Elisha's servant saw the Aramean army surrounding their city, he was overwhelmed with fear. But Elisha, aware of God's presence, prayed, "Open his eyes, Lord, so that he may see." God opened the servant's eyes to reveal the hills full of horses and chariots of fire—God's heavenly army—surrounding and protecting them. Instead of focusing on the enemy's power, the servant was reminded of God's greater strength and presence.

GOD'S PRESENCE AND POWER

Psalm 46:1-7 reminds us of God's unwavering presence and power, offering peace, strength, and joy even in the face of life's greatest challenges. Here are four truths that highlight His faithfulness and provide encouragement for our daily lives.

GOD IS OUR REFUGE AND STRENGTH

- The passage begins by declaring God as a safe place and a source of power, reminding us that He is always present and ready to help in times of trouble.

WE DO NOT NEED TO FEAR

- Even when the earth shakes and the mountains crumble, this Psalm assures us that God's sovereignty and stability give us confidence to face our challenges.

THE RIVER BRINGS JOY

- Unlike the chaos of the roaring seas, the river in verse 4 symbolizes peace, provision, and the gladness that comes from being in God's presence.

GOD IS ALWAYS WITH US

- Whether protecting the city of God or helping us in our daily struggles, God's presence is a steadying force that keeps us from falling (v. 5-7).

More Food for Thought...

Surely you have granted him unending blessings and made him glad with the joy of Your presence.
–Psalm 21:6

And those the Lord has rescued will return. They will enter Zion with singing; everlasting joy will crown their heads. Gladness and joy will overtake them, and sorrow and sighing will flee away.
– Isaiah 35:10

In Him our hearts rejoice, for we trust in His holy name.
–Psalm 33:21

I will be glad and rejoice in You; I will sing the praises of Your name, O Most High.
– Psalm 9:2

Sing, Daughter Zion; shout aloud, Israel! Be glad and rejoice with all your heart, Daughter Jerusalem!
– Zephaniah 3:14

Thoughts
and Jots

3
THE SOURCE OF OUR JOY

> *I am the vine; you are the branches. If you remain in me and I in you, you will bear much fruit; apart from me you can do nothing.*
>
> —John 15:5

In the fall of 2019, we were hit with a blizzard unlike any I'd seen in years. Heavy, wet snow covered the province, snapping power lines and plunging thousands of homes into darkness. I remember it well. My daughter, Maddy, had a newborn baby at the time. While the rest of our family was safe by the warmth of a fire, she was doing her best to keep the baby warm and fed in the dark.

After several hours, with no end in sight, they packed up the baby, drove an hour through the storm, and stepped into the safety of our home. That night, as we sat by the fire, I was reminded how much we take power for granted.

Without it, the simplest things become impossible. There's no light to see, no heat to warm us, and no way to cook food. Even charging a phone or making a call is a challenge. Life without power is uncomfortable at best and dangerous at worst.

This reliance on power mirrors our need to be connected to Christ, the source of our power, strength, and joy. Jesus reminds us in John 15:5, "I am the vine; you are the branches. If you remain [abide] in me and I in you, you will bear much fruit; apart from me you can do nothing." What is this fruit that Jesus is talking about? Galatians 5:22-23 lists joy alongside love, peace, patience, and other virtues as the fruit of the Spirit, reflecting God's work in a believer's life.

Sure, we can try to manufacture a sense of joy by chasing the things that please us, but what happens when those things are out of reach? What happens when we're left disappointed, broken-hearted, unemployed, or rejected? If we're depending on the world to make us happy, we'll be let down time and again. But is that really what we want—to be happy one day and discouraged the next? God has a better plan for our lives than we could ever imagine: an abundant life steeped in peace and abounding in joy. Joy that isn't dependent on the ever-changing world. Joy that flows from the Spirit within, bringing light to even our darkest days.

Don’t take that power for granted. Don't wait for a crisis to seek that connection. Joy thrives when we're connected to Christ. If we hope to remain in that joy, it starts by abiding in Christ. Spend time in prayer, dig into God's Word, and surrender your worries to Him. When we cultivate this connection, joy becomes a natural part of our life in good times and bad. The world can't offer the unshakable joy that comes from the Spirit—but when we're connected to Christ, we have access to joy that nothing and no one can take.

WHAT IT MEANS TO "ABIDE" IN CHRIST

Abiding in Christ is the foundation of a fruitful and joyful Christian life. James 4:8 gives us insight into how to abide, saying, "Come near to God and he will come near to you. Wash your hands, you sinners, and purify your hearts, you double-minded." This verse reveals that abiding in Christ requires both inward and outward change:

OUTWARD CHANGE

"Washing our hands" symbolizes righteous living. It involves turning from sin and aligning our actions with God's Word. This outward change reflects our commitment to Christ.

INWARD CHANGE

"Purifying our hearts" refers to surrendering sinful desires and cultivating devotion to God. John writes, "Do not love the world or anything in the world..." (1 John 2:15-16, NIV). Rejecting worldly desires allows us to draw closer to God.

DRAWING NEAR TO GOD

Abiding in Christ happens as we seek Him through prayer, repentance, and His Word. 1 John 2:6 sums it up well by saying, "Whoever claims to live in him must live as Jesus did." By living this way, we experience His strength, love, and joy daily.

READ AND REFLECT

Read John 15:1-12. How does abiding in Christ bring a joy that is different from what the world offers?

3 WAYS TO CULTIVATE JOY

1. CREATE SOMETHING: USE YOUR CREATIVITY TO MAKE ART, WRITE, OR BAKE AS AN ACT OF WORSHIP.
2. CLING TO GOD'S PROMISES: MEMORIZE VERSES LIKE ROMANS 8:28 TO REMIND YOURSELF OF HIS FAITHFULNESS.
3. LAUGH OFTEN: LET JOY OVERFLOW BY EMBRACING LIGHTHEARTED MOMENTS AND A CHEERFUL HEART.

LET'S MAP IT OUT

the source of life and sustenance for believers

dependant on the vine for nourishment and growth

I am the vine; you are the branches. If you

Greek word "μένω" (meno) meaning "to stay, dwell, or abide

remain in me and I in you,

spiritual actions and qualities that glorify God.

you will bear much fruit;

Dependant on Christ for spiritual growth

apart from me you can do nothing.

John 15:5, NIV

Bearing fruit is evidence of faith and connection to Christ (Matthew 7:16-20)

"Remain in Him" requires yielding control of our lives to Jesus

More Food for Thought...

I delight greatly in the Lord; my soul rejoices in my God. For He has clothed me with garments of salvation and arrayed me in a robe of His righteousness.
– Isaiah 61:10

Now is your time of grief, but I will see you again and you will rejoice, and no one will take away your joy.
– John 16:22

But may the righteous be glad and rejoice before God; may they be happy and joyful.
– Psalm 68:3

Rejoice in the Lord always. I will say it again: Rejoice!
–Philippians 4:4

The Lord makes firm the steps of the one who delights in Him.
– Psalm 37:23

Thoughts
and Jots

4

JOY COMES IN THE MORNING

> *Weeping may stay for the night, but rejoicing comes in the morning.*
>
> —Psalm 30:5

I used to sew. A lot. In the mid-70s, we had a small fabric store in our basement while my uncle's business was being renovated. Later, in high school, I sewed furry dice—a fun family project where everyone helped cut, stuff, and stitch the trendy fad.

By the time my first son was born, I was into quilt making. I loved the creativity, the patterns, and the satisfaction of completing a project. But once the kids started crawling, I put away my sewing supplies. For the most part, they've been retired ever since.

These days, when I do sew, I find I'm a bit lost. It's just not the same without my Singer 66. That machine was like an old friend—I knew its quirks and how to fix them. It only did straight stitches and zigzags, but that's all I needed. Today's machines? They have too many features, and one problem after another seems to arise. If it's not the tension, it's the thread. If not the thread, it’s the bobbin. Sometimes I thread it wrong—or maybe it's me.

Life can feel a lot like that sewing machine, can't it? Tangled problems, unexpected frustrations, and challenges that make you want to give up.

Whether it's tension in relationships, loose ends at work, or a knot in your heart you can't seem to undo, life's struggles can feel overwhelming at times. Like trying to thread a needle with shaky hands, some days nothing seems to go right.

But here's the thing: when I get past the new learning curve, troubleshoot a few problems, and stay the course, I discover there's beauty at the end of persistence and patience. So it is with life, sometimes things get harder before they get better. Psalm 30:5 reminds us, "Weeping may stay for the night, but rejoicing comes in the morning."

This verse doesn't deny life's hardships; it acknowledges them. Nights of weeping, frustration, and pain are real. But they won't last forever. God's promises assure us that joy is coming. Like the dawn breaking after a dark night, His faithfulness brings light, renewal, and rejoicing.

In hindsight, I see how God has worked in my life. How He comforted me, how He strengthened me, how He went before me, and how He walked through the fire with me. As much as I wanted instant relief from my sorrow and pain, the resolution came in His way and His time. Those seasons of darkness were God's way of refining, teaching, and preparing me for the joy that comes to those who faithfully trust Him.

If you're in a season of weeping, my friend, remember, it's always darkest just before the dawn. The morning is near and with it comes joy. How do I know that? Because the same God that's been faithful to you in the past will be just as faithful to you in the future. Amen? Hold onto that truth and carry it with you through the darkness.

Remember the times when He turned your mourning into rejoicing, and hold onto those moments of hope. Life may feel uncertain now, but God is at work—creating something beautiful, even if you can't see it yet. Joy comes in the morning, my friend. Hold on. The dawn is near.

READ AND REFLECT

Read Matthew 14:22-33. How does Jesus' presence during the disciples' darkest hours encourage you to trust Him during your own life's storms?

P.S. As you were reading that story, did you notice what time of day it took place?

EVEN WHEN LIFE FEELS OVERWHELMING, GOD IS AT WORK. TRUST HIS TIMING, HOLD ONTO HIS PROMISES, AND REMEMBER—JOY COMES IN THE MORNING.

WORDS TO GROW BY

If you ever find yourself lost in a sea of uncertainty, about to lose hope, remember this: When the disciples were stuck in the storm, Jesus showed up, walking on water, and reminded them He was in control: "Take courage! It is I. Don't be afraid" (Matthew 14:27). Just like that, He shows up for us too. Life can feel overwhelming, and the night can feel endless, but morning always comes. Even when we can't see the way forward, He is working behind the scenes, guiding us through. Jesus brings calm in the chaos and hope in the hardest moments, proving that joy is never far behind. Hold on to this truth: no matter how dark it feels in the moment, His faithfulness will bring joy in the morning.

3 WAYS TO CULTIVATE JOY

1. PRACTICE GRATITUDE: KEEP A JOURNAL AND WRITE DOWN THREE BLESSINGS EACH DAY.
2. ENCOURAGE SOMEONE: SEND A KIND NOTE, TEXT, OR SMALL GIFT TO BRIGHTEN SOMEONE'S DAY.
3. REST IN GOD'S PRESENCE: DEDICATE TIME TO QUIETLY SIT WITH HIM AND REFLECT ON HIS LOVE.

PERSONAL REFLECTION

Can you recall a time when God turned your sorrow into joy? What happened, and how does His faithfulness in that moment strengthen your trust in Him for the future?

LET'S MAP IT OUT

A time of sorrow, grief, or trials

Weeping may stay

Temporary, not permanent

Represents darkness, struggles or difficult seasons

for the night, but rejoicing

Joy, restoration, or a renewed spirit

comes in the morning.

A promise, inevitable hope!

Psalm 30:5, NIV

Denotes a new beginning. Relief from darkness.

More Food for Thought...

The desert and the parched land will be glad; the wilderness will rejoice and blossom. Like the crocus, it will burst into bloom; it will rejoice greatly and shout for joy.
– Isaiah 35:1-2

Our mouths were filled with laughter, our tongues with songs of joy. Then it was said among the nations, 'The Lord has done great things for them.'
– Psalm 126:2

Joy and gladness will be found in her, thanksgiving and the sound of singing.
– Isaiah 51:3

Light shines on the righteous and joy on the upright in heart.
– Psalm 97:11

The prospect of the righteous is joy, but the hopes of the wicked come to nothing.
– Proverbs 10:28

Thoughts and Jots

5

TRUTH LEADS TO JOY

> *Then you will know the truth, and the truth will set you free.*
>
> —John 8:32

One summer, we were out at family Bible camp. I was already a mom by this time, and my parents had joined us for the week. It was one of those beautiful, memory-making trips where you reconnect with family, laugh around campfires, and leave the world behind.

Then we heard about the haunted house.

It was just up the hill and through the trees, they said. My sister and her husband warned us not to go, which, of course, only made my dad and me want to check it out even more. "We're not afraid of an old house," I told them. "Besides, we don't believe in ghosts—other than the Holy Ghost—and He's not about to jump out and scare us!"

And so, the two of us set off on a hike to find this mysterious house.

The closer we got to the hill, the more I began to feel uneasy. The trees seemed darker; the air thicker. What would we find up there? And why were people afraid to go near it?

Just as I began to wonder if we should turn back, something large rustled in the bushes. A thick, bushy tree began to sway violently. My heart was racing as something big moved toward us.

Whatever it was, I didn't want to stick around to find out. My dad ran, scaling an old wooden fence in record time, yelling as he passed me. I followed, nearly tripping over my own feet. And, just as I was about to leap over the fence, our "monster" emerged from the bushes.

A big, old, white cow.

There it stood, chewing her cud and minding her own business.

I froze for a moment, staring at this harmless animal before bursting into laughter. By the time I caught up to my dad, I was in tears from laughing so hard. Both of us had been scared off by an innocent cow. We laughed until our sides hurt, and for the rest of the week, it became the running joke in our family. Every time someone brought it up, we couldn't help but laugh all over again, picturing my dad screaming while he ran up the hill.

Fear grows in the absence of truth. It thrives on the unknown, exaggerations in our minds, and assumptions that aren't grounded in reality. Fear has a way of consuming our thoughts, robbing us of the joy and peace that God desires for us.

When we allow fear to take root, it distorts our perspective and magnifies our worries. But truth has the power to shrink fear. As Jesus says in John 8:32 (NIV), *"Then you will know the truth, and the truth will set you free."* Truth brings freedom—not just freedom from sin, but freedom from the grip of fear that keeps us from living a joyfully spirit-filled life.

PRACTICALLY SPEAKING

Did you know that the Bible is filled with over 7,000 promises from God? That's over 7,000 reminders of His faithfulness and steadfast love! By clinging to these promises, we can rest in the assurance that He is our protector, provider, and guide. Truth doesn't just push fear aside—it transforms it. Peace calms our anxiety, and joy replaces even the deepest sorrow. As Psalm 119:165 says, "Great peace have those who love your law, and nothing can make them stumble." If you're not doing it already, find a quiet corner in your home and make Bible study a regular part of your daily routine. Even just a few minutes in God's Word can make a big difference in your day.

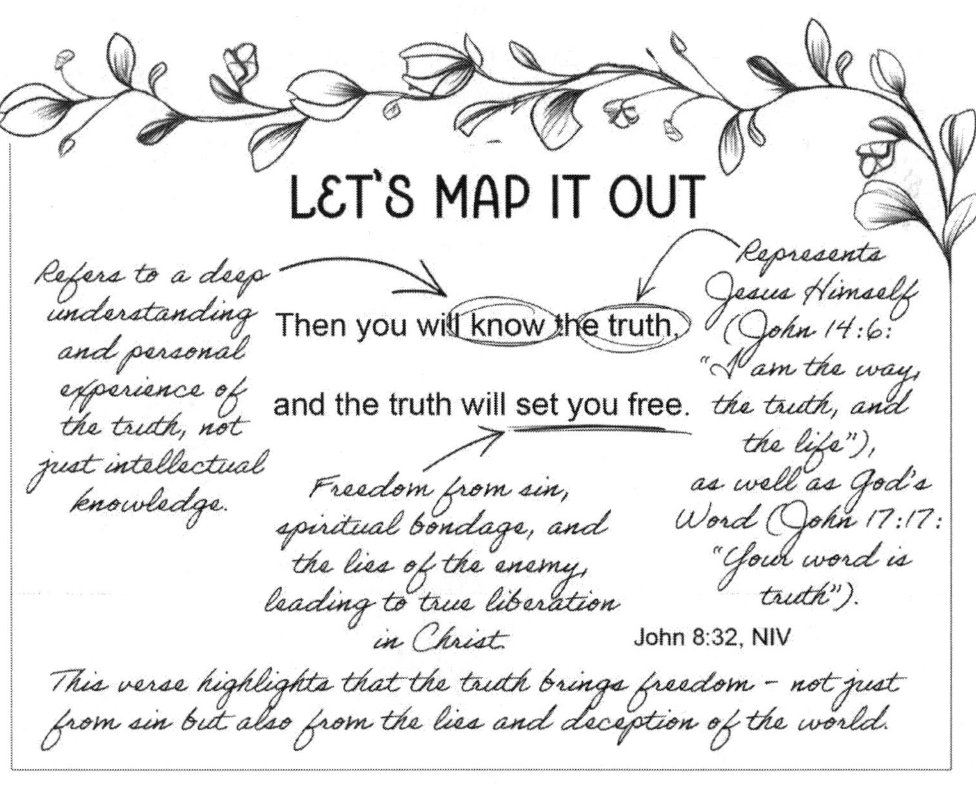

Read Psalm 119:41–48. What are some ways the psalmist actively seeks and engages with God's truth?

Read Psalm 119:49-56. What are some ways the psalmist finds comfort and strength in God's Word?

20 Promises from God That Bring Us Joy

Highlight these in your Bible!

1. He will never leave us nor forsake us (Deut. 31:6).
2. We are His children (John 1:12).
3. He has plans to prosper us, not harm us (Jeremiah 29:11).
4. His peace surpasses all understanding (Philippians 4:7).
5. He will strengthen us when we are weak (Isaiah 41:10).
6. His mercies are new every morning (Lamentations 3:22-23).
7. He is faithful to forgive our sins (1 John 1:9).
8. We have eternal life through Jesus (John 3:16).
9. He hears our prayers (1 John 5:14-15).
10. He works all things for good (Romans 8:28).
11. He is our refuge and strength (Psalm 46:1).
12. He will guide us continually (Isaiah 58:11).
13. He will provide for all our needs (Philippians 4:19).
14. His love casts out fear (1 John 4:18).
15. He renews our strength (Isaiah 40:31).
16. He will fight for us (Exodus 14:14).
17. We are more than conquerors through Him (Romans 8:37).
18. He is with us in every trial (Isaiah 43:2).
19. Nothing can separate us from His love (Romans 8:39).
20. He gives us fullness of joy in His presence (Psalm 16:11).

More Food for Thought...

Your statutes are my heritage forever; they are the joy of my heart.
– Psalm 119:111

Surely God is my salvation; I will trust and not be afraid. The Lord, the Lord Himself, is my strength and my defense; He has become my salvation. With joy you will draw water from the wells of salvation.
– Isaiah 12:2-3

Blessed are those who find wisdom, those who gain understanding.
– Proverbs 3:13

But the one who looks intently into the perfect law of freedom, and continues to do so—not being a forgetful hearer, but an effective doer—he will be blessed in what he does.
–James 1:25

The precepts of the Lord are right, giving joy to the heart.
– Psalm 19:8

Thoughts and Jots

6

HE IS GREATER THAN OUR STRUGGLES

> *Glorify the Lord with me; let us exalt his name together.*
>
> —Psalm 34:3

Have you ever had one of those moments where your perception suddenly shifts? When something you thought was real was just a matter of perspective? That happened to me yesterday when my daughter brought over her two little pugs, for a visit. At least I used to think they were little. For years, Oliver and Sadie, were dwarfed by our Bull Mastiff, Gabby, who passed away a couple of months ago.

After her passing, my husband Michael bought me a Yorkshire Terrier. If you've never seen a Yorkie, picture an adorable squirrel with a big bark. Sawyer is so small that my grandchildren want to put him in the dollhouse. One day, I couldn't find him and after searching everywhere, I saw two little eyes peeking out of the dollhouse window. He's a character, to say the least.

Two months into living with Sawyer, my daughter brought Sadie and Oliver over for a visit. But, here's the thing—the moment they walked through the door, I was stunned. These "little" pugs I'd always thought of as tiny were towering, muscular dogs in comparison to my pint-sized

Yorkie. They hadn't changed, but my perception of them had. What I thought was "small" wasn't small at all — at least not anymore.

That got me thinking about the power of perception, and how deceitful it can be. Problems we face often seem enormous because we're so close to them. We magnify our struggles, seeing them as towering giants, and in the process, we shrink God in our minds. But God hasn't changed. He's still the Creator of the universe, the One who speaks and calms the storm, the One who can do immeasurably more than we ask or imagine (Ephesians 3:20).

When we're consumed by the size of our problems, we need a shift in perspective. Psalm 34:3 says, "Glorify the Lord with me; let us exalt his name together." The word "exalt" means to magnify or make bigger in our hearts and minds. This doesn't mean we change the size of God — He's already infinite. But when we focus on Him, His greatness, and His faithfulness, our perception shifts, and our problems fall into their proper place.

Just like I saw those pugs differently after being around Sawyer, spending time in God's Word and in prayer can help us see our circumstances differently. The problems that seemed insurmountable before pale in comparison to the God we serve. He's bigger than our struggles, and He's already gone ahead of us to make a way.

So, what's clouding your joy today? Are you magnifying the problem or magnifying God? Take a moment to shift your focus, remembering that He is greater than anything you face. The next time your perception makes a small thing look big, remind yourself that your God is bigger.

THE POWER OF PERSPECTIVE

The story of David and Goliath (1 Samuel 17) teaches us how the right perspective can change everything. When the Israelites saw Goliath, they magnified his size and strength. David, on the other hand, chose to magnify the Lord. This shift in perspective gave him the confidence to face the giant.

MAGNIFYING THE PROBLEM

The Israelites were consumed by fear. They saw Goliath as an unbeatable giant, focusing only on his size, his strength, and his threats. Their perception of the problem overwhelmed their faith and paralyzed them into inaction. "On hearing the Philistine's words, Saul and all the Israelites were dismayed and terrified." —1 Samuel 17:11 (NIV)

MAGNIFYING GOD

David saw the same giant, but his perspective was different. He magnified God's power instead of the enemy's strength. David remembered God's faithfulness, saying, "The Lord who rescued me from the paw of the lion and the paw of the bear will rescue me from the hand of this Philistine" (1 Samuel 17:37).

VICTORY THROUGH FAITH

With just a sling and a stone, David defeated Goliath. His victory wasn't because of his own strength but because of his trust in God. David's story reminds us that when we focus on God's power, no challenge is too great.
"All those gathered here will know that it is not by sword or spear that the Lord saves; for the battle is the Lord's, and he will give all of you into our hands." —1 Samuel 17:47 (NIV)

READ AND REFLECT

Whenever we're facing worry and doubt, we can shift our perspective, just like David did, by remembering who God is. Read the following verses and write down what you know about God beside each one:

Psalm 46:1

Jeremiah 32:17

Isaiah 41:10

Jeremiah 29:11

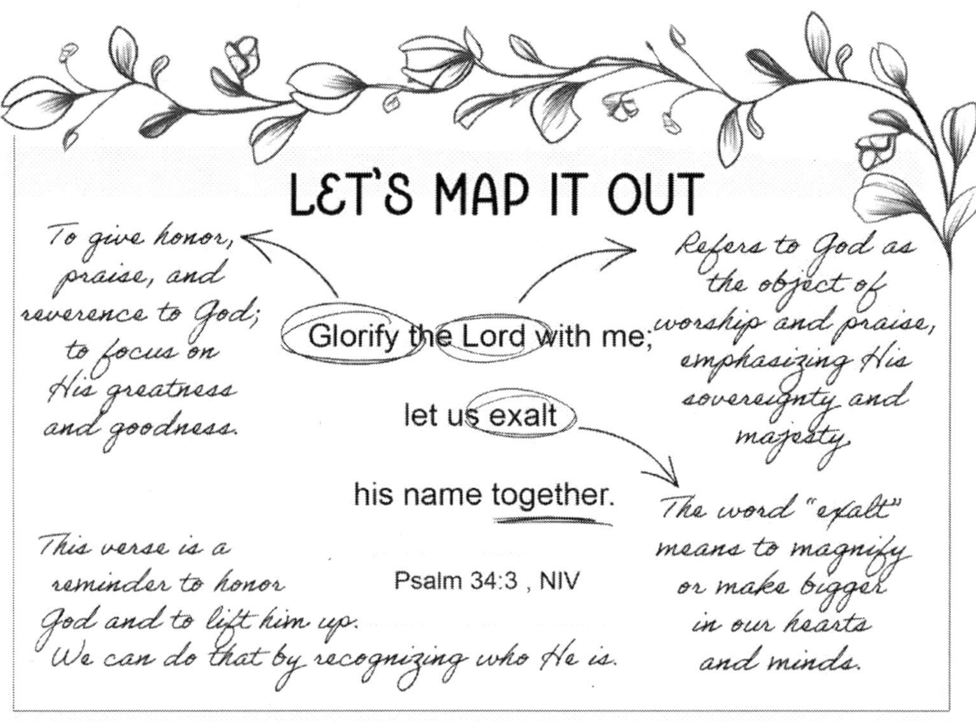

Your sorrow itself shall be turned into joy. Not the sorrow to be taken away, and joy to be put in its place, but the very sorrow which now grieves you shall be turned into joy. God not only takes away the bitterness and gives sweetness in its place, but turns the bitterness into sweetness itself.

- Charles H. Spurgeon

More Food for Thought...

What then shall we say in response to these things? If God is for us, who can be against us?
– Romans 8:31

So we say with confidence: "The Lord is my helper; I will not be afraid. What can man do to me?"
– Hebrews 3:16

Now to him who is able to do immeasurably more than all we ask or imagine, according to his power that is at work within us, to him be glory in the church and in Christ Jesus throughout all generations, for ever and ever! Amen.
– Ephesians 3:20-21

Jesus looked at them and said, "With man this is impossible, but with God all things are possible."
– Matthew 19:6

The LORD is on my side; I will not be afraid. What can man do to me?
– Psalm 118:6

Thoughts and Jots

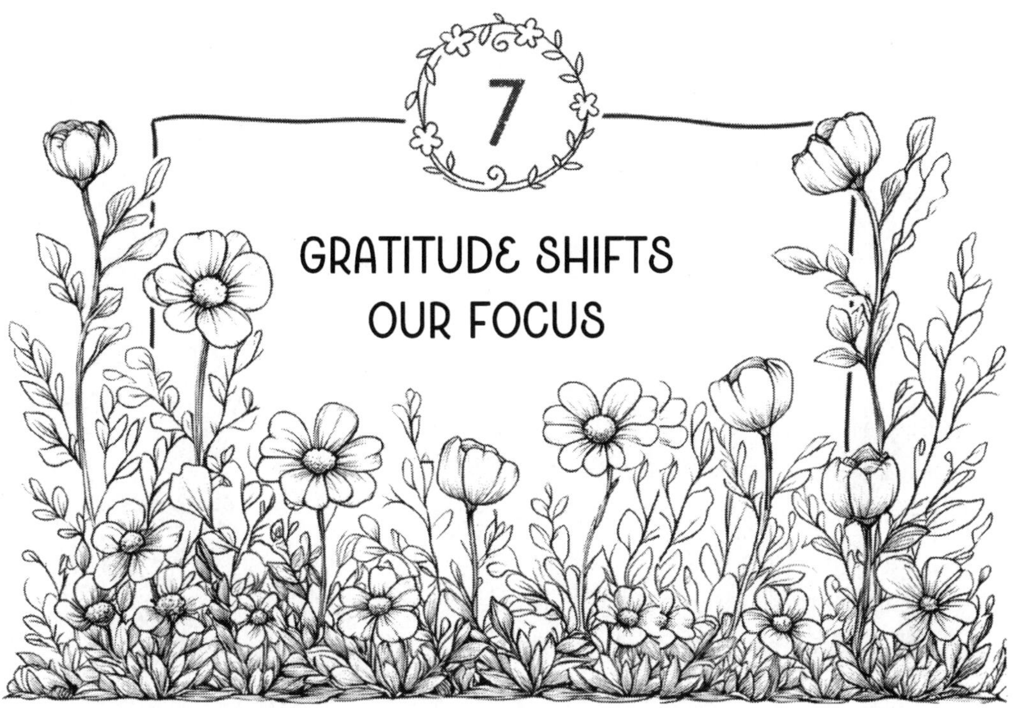

7

GRATITUDE SHIFTS OUR FOCUS

I love sunshine. There's something about the warmth on my face and the brilliance of light that brings joy to my heart. In fact, when we bought our car last year, I told my husband I didn't care what kind of car he picked as long as it had a sunroof. There's just nothing like opening the roof to let the sunshine flood in. The long days of summer are my favorite, especially here in Manitoba, where the sun doesn't go to sleep until after 10 p.m.

> *Rejoice always, pray continually, give thanks in all circumstances; for this is God's will for you in Christ Jesus.*
>
> —1 Thess. 5:16-18

Cloudy days, on the other hand, are a mixed bag for me. I don't mind the fluffy white clouds that float lazily across a blue sky—they're like nature's artwork. But those thick, heavy clouds that block out the sun? I could do without them. They make everything feel a little dimmer, a little heavier.

Isn't life like that sometimes? We have sunny days when everything feels bright and full of possibility, and then we have cloudy days when the weight of the world seems to press in. It's easy to let the clouds take over, to let worries and frustrations block our view of the good things around us. But here's the thing—gratitude can be the key to shifting our perspective.

Gratitude shifts our focus away from this world and back onto Christ. It reminds us of all that we have and how much we are loved. It dissipates clouds and invites the sun to break through. Gratitude changes our attitude, thus changing our day! When we take time to thank God for His blessings—even small ones like sunshine or a warm cup of coffee—we open the door to joy.

The Bible says, "Rejoice always, pray continually, give thanks in all circumstances; for this is God's will for you in Christ Jesus" (1 Thessalonians 5:16-18, NIV). Notice that gratitude isn't just for the sunny days. It's for the cloudy ones too. When we thank God in the middle of life's storms, we're acknowledging that He is still in control, that He is still good, and that He is still working all things together for our good.

So how do we cultivate gratitude on cloudy days? Start small. Write down three things you're thankful for every morning. Pause to thank God for the beauty of creation, the kindness of a friend, or the simple joy of a favorite song. Gratitude isn't about pretending everything is perfect; it's about recognizing that God's goodness is present in every moment.

Just like a sunroof can bring a little light into a car, gratitude can bring a little joy into our lives. It doesn't chase away every storm, but it does give us the strength to face them with hope. Let's make it a habit to look for the sunshine—even when the clouds try to block our view.

READ AND REFLECT

Read Acts 16:16-34. Paul and Silas chose to pray and sing hymns despite their painful circumstances. What can we learn from their response to trials about cultivating gratitude and joy?

3 WAYS TO CULTIVATE JOY

1. MEDITATE ON GOD'S CHARACTER: REFLECT ON HIS MERCY, GRACE, AND STEADFAST LOVE.
2.
3. SPEND TIME OUTDOORS: TAKE A WALK OR SIT IN NATURE TO MARVEL AT GOD'S CREATION.
4. PRAY WITH GRATITUDE: BEGIN EACH PRAYER BY THANKING GOD FOR HIS BLESSINGS, BIG AND SMALL.

TODAY I'M THANKFUL FOR

Use the space below to list four things that you're thankful for.

1. ______________________________

2. ______________________________

3. ______________________________

4. ______________________________

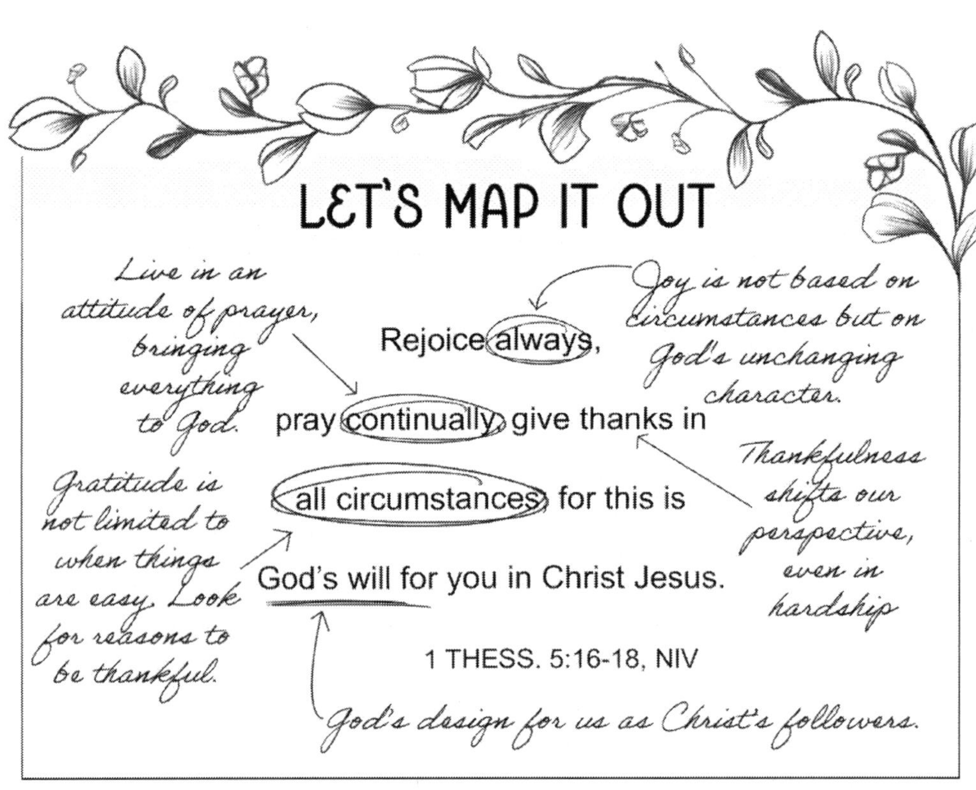

WHAT'S CLOUDING YOUR VIEW?

Can you think of a time when joy felt far away? What challenges were clouding your view of God's goodness? And how might practicing gratitude have opened the door to joy?

More Food for Thought...

In that day they will say, 'Surely this is our God; we trusted in Him, and He saved us. This is the Lord, we trusted in Him; let us rejoice and be glad in His salvation.'
– Isaiah 25:9

The righteous will rejoice in the Lord and take refuge in Him; all the upright in heart will glory in Him!
– Psalm 64:10

Be glad, people of Zion, rejoice in the Lord your God, for He has given you the autumn rains because He is faithful.
– Joel 2:23

And my spirit rejoices in God my Savior.
– Luke 1:47

Sing joyfully to the Lord, you righteous; it is fitting for the upright to praise Him.
– Psalm 33:1

Thoughts
and Jots

8

WALKING AND LEAPING AND PRAISING GOD

It's been years—a whole lot of years—but you never forget your first publishing contract. It all began with an interview I did for Christian Women Online Magazine, which opened the door to an exciting opportunity I hadn't anticipated.

The journey was fun, but not without challenges. Finding the right publisher took months—months filled with hope, uncertainty, and countless prayers. If there's one thing I clung to during that time, it was the power of prayer. I spent that season on my knees, pouring my heart out to God and trusting Him to lead the way.

Looking back, it's clear that those moments of waiting weren't wasted. They were a time of preparation, teaching me to rely on God more fully and to find joy in the process, not just the result. Often, we want answers right away, but God uses seasons of waiting to grow us in ways we wouldn't choose on our own. It's in those moments that we learn to lean into His faithfulness, trusting that He's doing a good work even when we can't yet see it.

> *May the God of hope fill you with all joy and peace as you trust in him, so that you may overflow with hope by the power of the Holy Spirit.*
>
> —Romans 15:13

Romans 15:13 says, "May the God of hope fill you with all joy and peace as you trust in him, so that you may overflow with hope by the power of the Holy Spirit." That verse perfectly captures what I felt during that season. My prayers, though filled with longing, were also filled with trust. I learned that joy and peace come not from the outcomes we hope for, but from surrendering to God's perfect will.

Eventually, the moment I had been waiting for came. One day, the phone rang with the news I'd been praying for—I had a publishing contract! I'll never forget the joy and hilarity of that moment. In my excitement, I bolted down the basement stairs to share the news with my son, tripped on a toy, and landed flat on my back. But even that didn't stop me. I jumped up, laughing at myself, and kept running to share the good news.

Whenever I think of that night, I'm reminded of the man who was healed in Acts 3:8. The Bible tells us, "Then he went with them into the temple courts, walking and jumping, and praising God." His joy wasn't quiet or contained—it was a bold declaration of what God had done.

True joy isn't just about answered prayers or things going our way. It's about recognizing God's presence and faithfulness throughout the journey. Joy rises when we trust Him, not because everything is perfect, but because He is with us. It's the kind of joy that makes you laugh at yourself, stumble in excitement, and boldly proclaim, "Look at what God has done!" That's the beauty of joy—it's an outward expression of an inward trust in God's goodness. It's a reminder that His promises are true, and His love is unchanging.

READ AND REFLECT

Read Acts 3:1-10. The people around the lame man noticed both his healing and his joy. What can the man's actions teach us about the way we respond to God's blessings?

LET'S MAP IT OUT

God doesn't just offer us hope— He is the source of our hope. *God is filling us* *complete, abundant measure*

May the God of hope fill you with all
joy and peace as you trust in him,

Joy = charaa (strong's 5479) a deep, abiding sense of joy and gladness that is rooted in spiritual realities rather than external circumstances.

an active, ongoing process of surrendering our worries to God.

so that you may overflow with hope by
the power of the Holy Spirit.

the purpose is to overflow and impact others.

Hope is generated by the Holy Spirit

—ROMANS 15:13

10 Reasons We Should Let Joy Overflow

1. **JOY IS A POWERFUL TESTIMONY OF GOD'S WORK IN OUR LIVES.**
   THE HEALED MAN'S JOY CAUSED PEOPLE TO BE AMAZED AND RECOGNIZE GOD'S POWER.
2. **OVERFLOWING JOY POINTS OTHERS TO THE SOURCE OF TRUE HOPE.**
   OUR JOY AND PEACE ARE MEANT TO OVERFLOW BY THE POWER OF THE HOLY SPIRIT, INSPIRING OTHERS TO SEEK CHRIST.
3. **JOY IS CONTAGIOUS AND INSPIRES OTHERS.**
   A CHEERFUL HEART BRINGS JOY TO OTHERS. WHEN WE SHARE OUR JOY, IT LIFTS THOSE AROUND US.
4. **OUR JOY GLORIFIES GOD.**
   WHEN GOD'S PEOPLE ARE FILLED WITH JOY, THEY GIVE GLORY TO HIM, AND OTHERS NOTICE HIS GOODNESS.
5. **SHARING JOY ENCOURAGES OTHERS THROUGH DIFFICULT TIMES.**
   GOD COMFORTS US SO THAT WE CAN COMFORT OTHERS. OUR JOY CAN OFFER HOPE TO THOSE WHO ARE STRUGGLING.
6. **OVERFLOWING JOY SHOWS GRATITUDE TO GOD FOR HIS BLESSINGS.**
   THE HEALED LEPER RETURNED TO JESUS, PRAISING GOD IN A LOUD VOICE, AS AN EXPRESSION OF GRATITUDE.

7. **IT FULFILLS OUR CALLING TO BE LIGHT IN THE WORLD.**
   WE ARE CALLED TO LET OUR LIGHT SHINE BEFORE OTHERS SO THEY MAY SEE OUR GOOD DEEDS AND GLORIFY GOD.
8. **JOY BUILDS UP THE BODY OF CHRIST.**
   WHEN WE ENCOURAGE OTHERS WITH OUR JOY, WE STRENGTHEN THE FAITH AND UNITY OF BELIEVERS.
9. **IT REFLECTS THE FRUIT OF THE SPIRIT IN OUR LIVES.**
   JOY IS A FRUIT OF THE HOLY SPIRIT, AND LETTING IT OVERFLOW SHOWS THAT GOD IS AT WORK IN US.
10. **OUR JOY GIVES OTHERS A GLIMPSE OF GOD'S KINGDOM.**
    THE KINGDOM OF GOD IS NOT ABOUT MATERIAL THINGS BUT ABOUT RIGHTEOUSNESS, PEACE, AND JOY IN THE HOLY SPIRIT.

More Food for Thought...

Those who sow with tears will reap with songs of joy.
– Psalm 126:5

But you will rejoice in the Lord and glory in the Holy One of Israel.
– Isaiah 41:16

My lips will shout for joy when I sing praise to You—
I whom You have delivered.
– Psalm 71:23

We wait in hope for the Lord; He is our help and our shield. In Him our hearts rejoice, for we trust in His holy name.
– Psalm 33:20-21

Deceit is in the hearts of those who plot evil, but those who promote peace have joy.
– Proverbs 12:20

Thoughts
and Jots

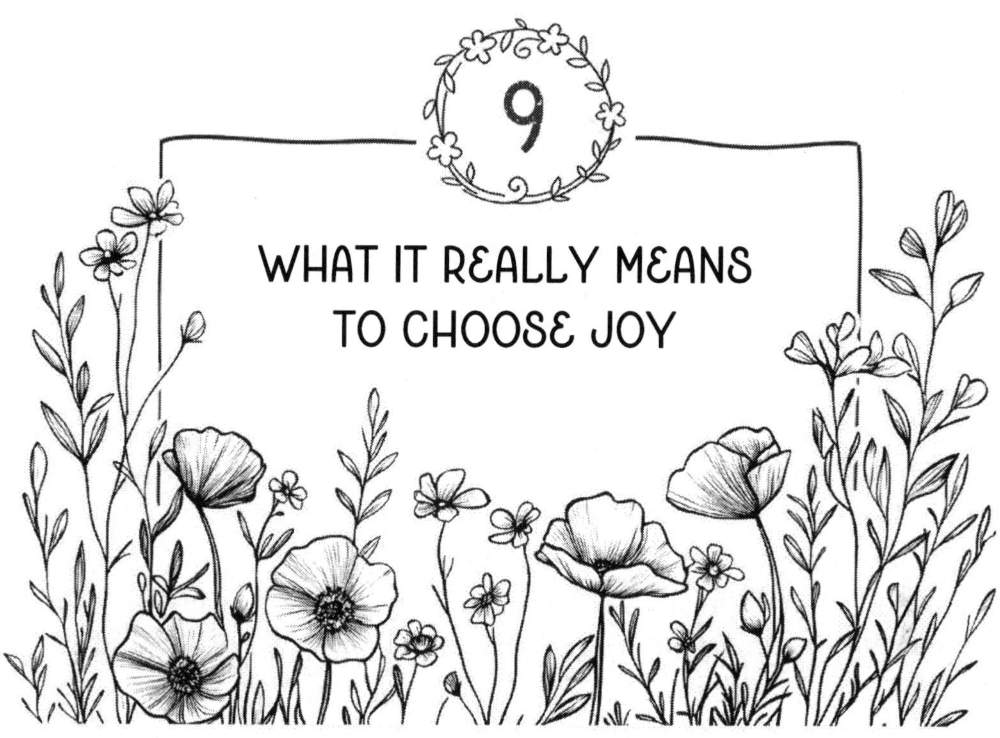

9

WHAT IT REALLY MEANS TO CHOOSE JOY

In times of deep sorrow, two little words can feel impossible at times: *choose joy.* Is it really that simple? Can I just *decide* to feel something I don't? It's almost as though people expect us to flip a switch and go from carrying deep hurt to radiating happiness, as if choosing joy means ignoring the weight of our pain. The idea feels almost dismissive of the depth of our pain. And yet, perhaps there's *more to those two words than meets the eye.*

When James writes, *"Consider it pure joy, my brothers and sisters, whenever you face trials of many kinds"* (James 1:2, NIV), he's not telling us to fake a smile or pretend everything is fine. The word *consider* invites us to take a different approach. It doesn't ask us to deny our pain but instead to shift our perspective.

> *Consider it pure joy, my brothers and sisters, whenever you face trials of many kinds.*
>
> —James 1:2

The Greek word for *consider* here, *hēgéomai,* implies leading or guiding our thoughts. In essence, James is encouraging us to *choose* how we interpret our circumstances. It's not about ignoring the reality of our trials but recognizing that joy and sorrow can coexist because of the hope we have in Christ.

Think of it as a hot air balloon. Life's trials are heavy and burdensome, like sandbags weighing us down. But when we fix our eyes on God's promises and release those weights—fear, anger, doubt—we can rise above our sorrow. Joy doesn't erase the storm; it simply lifts us high enough to see the bigger picture.

Joy isn't about plastering on a happy face; it's a deep-seated confidence in God's goodness and faithfulness, even when life feels anything but good. This type of joy is rooted in knowing that our trials have a purpose. James goes on to explain that trials produce perseverance, which leads to spiritual maturity (James 1:3-4). Joy, then, isn't about *feeling* good but about trusting God's ability to bring good from the hardest moments.

This shift in perspective doesn't come naturally—it takes intentional effort. It might look like finding gratitude in small blessings or leaning into God's promises when fear threatens to overwhelm us. It's not about denying the pain; it's a decision to rise above it, fixing our thoughts on His faithfulness instead of letting our thoughts bring us down. Trusting that even when we don't see it, God is at work.

Over time, I've come to see that joy isn't about what I feel; it's about Who I trust. When I anchor my hope in Christ, joy becomes less of a fleeting emotion and more of a steadfast assurance.

So, is it simple? No. But is it possible? Yes—because joy isn't something we create; it's something that flows from within us when we fix our eyes on the Lord.

READ AND REFLECT

Read Habakkuk 3:17-19. Habakkuk shows us what it looks like to trust God with a heart that says, 'Even if life falls apart, I will rejoice in the Lord.' Take a moment to write your own 'even if' prayer in a similar fashion, reflecting on how you can choose to trust and rejoice in God no matter what challenges you may face.

NO SOUL THAT SERIOUSLY AND CONSTANTLY DESIRES JOY WILL EVER MISS IT. THOSE WHO SEEK FIND. TO THOSE WHO KNOCK IT IS OPENED.

—C.S. LEWIS

JOY IN THE SIMPLE THINGS

Use the space below to list five things that have brought you joy this past week:

1. ________________________________

2. ________________________________

3. ________________________________

4. ________________________________

5. ________________________________

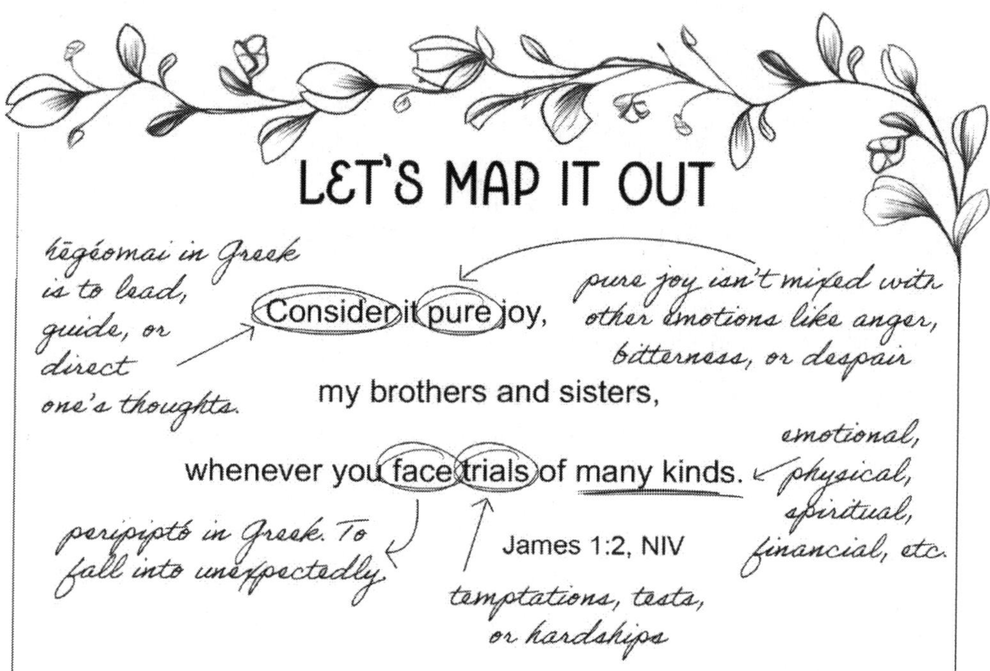

HANNAH CHOSE JOY

In 1 Samuel 1, we read about Hannah, a woman who knew the ache of waiting. She longed for a child, yet year after year, her prayers seemed to go unanswered. On top of that, she faced ridicule from those around her. But here's what stands out—Hannah didn't give up. She poured her heart out to God, trusting Him with her deepest pain. And her joy? It came *before* her circumstances changed. After praying, she worshiped, knowing God was faithful even in the waiting. Later, in 1 Samuel 2:1, she declared, "My heart rejoices in the Lord; in the Lord my horn is lifted high." Her story reminds us that real joy isn't rooted in what we receive, it's in trusting God's perfect timing and unfailing goodness.

More Food for Thought...

In all this you greatly rejoice, though now for a little while you may have had to suffer grief in all kinds of trials. These have come so that the proven genuineness of your faith—of greater worth than gold—may result in praise, glory, and honor when Jesus Christ is revealed.
–1 Peter 1:6-7

For our light and momentary troubles are achieving for us an eternal glory that far outweighs them all.
–2 Corinthians 4:17

Not only that, but we rejoice in our sufferings, knowing that suffering produces endurance, and endurance produces character, and character produces hope.
– Romans 5:3-4

For the Spirit God gave us does not make us timid, but gives us power, love, and self-discipline.
–2 Timothy 1:7

Thoughts
and Jots

Do you ever feel like you're at the end of your rope? You've done everything you know to do—planted seeds of kindness, read every marriage book on the shelf, prayed countless prayers for your prodigal children, or tried to show love to a difficult co-worker. And yet, nothing seems to change. The marriage remains distant, the children continue to wander, the difficult co-worker is still difficult, and your heart grows weary.

> *Those who go out weeping, carrying seed to sow, will return with songs of joy, carrying sheaves with them.*
>
> —Psalm 126:6

If this is where you find yourself today, you're not alone. Countless women (and men too, for that matter) carry the unseen weight of discouragement, wondering if their efforts have made any difference at all. They've shown grace, served their families, and poured out love with little or no return. After years of one-sided devotion, they question whether there's any point to pressing on.

Psalm 126:6 reminds us of the hope we have in God's promises: 'Those who go out weeping, carrying seed to sow, will return with songs of joy, carrying sheaves with them.' This verse paints a beautiful picture of perseverance—a farmer sowing his last bit of seed, tears streaming down his face, all the while trusting that a harvest will come. Though the season of planting may be painful, it holds the promise of joy when the harvest comes in.

In the same way, your efforts to love, forgive, and show kindness are seeds that God is using to accomplish His purposes. C.S. Lewis once said, 'Hardships often prepare ordinary people for an extraordinary destiny.' Your tears, prayers, and acts of faithfulness are not wasted—they are seeds of hope that God will water in His time. And even in the midst of those struggles, joy can be found—not in the resolution of your problems, but in the presence of the One who walks beside you.

Through times of waiting, seasons of uncertainty, and moments of doubt, Psalm 126:6 encourages us to keep going, even when we're weary. God sees our faithfulness. He hears our prayers. And He promises that our labor is not in vain.

So, how do we press on with joy when weariness sets in? By leaning into His strength and trusting that God is at work, even when you don't see it.

Take heart. The seeds you've planted are not forgotten. Keep showing up. Keep loving. Keep praying. And let God take it from there. When the harvest comes—and it will—you'll see that every act of kindness, every moment of grace, and every prayer whispered in faith was worth it.

Remember, dear friend, joy isn't the absence of hardship. It's the presence of God in the midst of it. He sees you, He loves you, and He is with you every step of the way.

READ AND REFLECT

Read Psalm 126. What was it about the Israelites' experience that impacted the nations around them? What can we learn from their example about the way we approach our freedom through Christ?

P.S. The word "fortunes" in Psalm 126 can be a little confusing because it doesn't mean wealth or material riches the way we might think today. Instead, it refers to God restoring what was lost— specifically, restoring the well-being, joy, and freedom of His people.

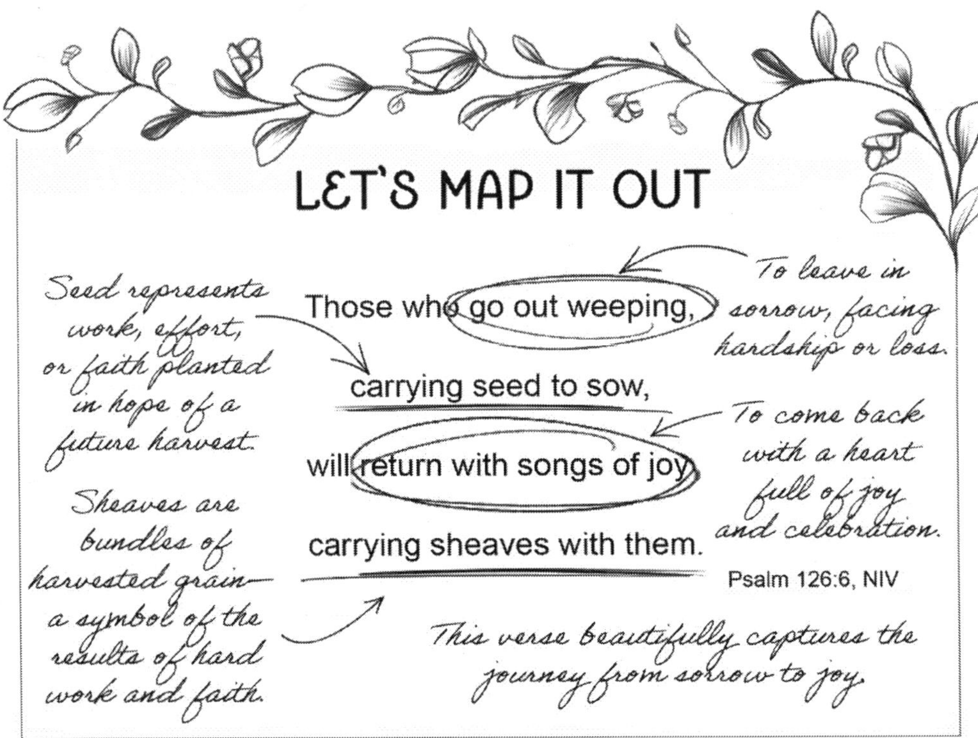

3 WAYS TO CULTIVATE JOY

1. RECOUNT PAST VICTORIES: REFLECT ON WAYS GOD HAS SHOWN HIS FAITHFULNESS IN YOUR LIFE.
2. WORSHIP DAILY: SING PRAISES TO GOD, EVEN IF IT'S JUST HUMMING ALONG TO A WORSHIP SONG.
3. RELEASE WORRY: SURRENDER YOUR ANXIETIES TO GOD AND TRUST IN HIS PERFECT TIMING.

GOD ISN'T FINISHED WITH YOU YET

The story of the Israelites in Babylonian captivity teaches us about perseverance. They had lost everything — their homes, their freedom, and their hope. Yet, even in exile, they held on to God's promises, trusting that He would restore them in His time.

SOWING IN FAITH

In captivity, the Israelites sowed seeds of faith through prayer, repentance, and obedience, even when their future seemed uncertain. They persevered, believing that God would fulfill His promises. Their story shows us that every act of faithfulness matters, even when we don't see immediate results.

WAITING IN HOPE

Waiting can be painful, but like the Israelites who endured seventy years of captivity, we are called to trust in God's faithfulness. The waiting season is never wasted. God is always at work behind the scenes, preparing a harvest we cannot yet see.

REAPING WITH JOY

Just as God restored the fortunes of the Israelites, He will complete the work He started in us. The harvest may not come right away, but every act of love and faith will be worth it.

Being confident of this, that he who began a good work in you will carry it on to completion until the day of Christ Jesus.

—PHILIPPIANS 1:6

More Food for Thought...

Let us not become weary in doing good, for at the proper time we will reap a harvest if we do not give up.
– Galatians 6:9

Sow your seed in the morning, and at evening let your hands not be idle, for you do not know which will succeed, whether this or that, or whether both will do equally well.
– Ecclesiastes 11:6

Therefore, my beloved brothers, be steadfast and immovable. Always excel in the work of the Lord, because you know that your labor in the Lord is not in vain.
– 1 Corinthians 15:58

Remember this: Whoever sows sparingly will also reap sparingly, and whoever sows generously will also reap generously.
– 2 Corinthians 9:6

Thoughts
and Jots

11

THE CHOICE TO BE BETTER NOT BITTER

> *All the days of the oppressed are wretched, but the cheerful heart has a continual feast.*
>
> —Proverbs 15:15

What is it about pouting that comes so naturally to us? Whether we're stuck in traffic, dealing with a harsh comment, or frustrated by plans falling through, we find ourselves giving in to the pull of the pout. We retreat into ourselves, fold our arms, and let the root of bitterness grow. But what if these moments of frustration are opportunities for something greater?

You've probably heard the story of Jonah and the big fish, but have you ever paid attention to his attitude after that? When God showed mercy to the people of Nineveh, Jonah wasn't exactly thrilled. Instead of rejoicing over their repentance, he sat down for a pity party of one. And it didn't stop there. In the final chapter of his story, Jonah found himself sitting outside the city, sulking over a withered plant. It's almost comical when you think about it—a grown man throwing a tantrum because his shade disappeared.

I'll admit, I see a bit of Jonah in myself. It's easy to let frustration get the better of us. We all have those moments when we say something we shouldn't, only to regret it later. But here's the thing about trials—they aren't meant to break us or make our lives miserable. They're designed to test our faith, to show us where we stand and give us a chance to grow. As Proverbs 15:15 says, "All the days of the oppressed are wretched, but the cheerful heart has a continual feast." When we choose joy, even in hard times, it changes everything.

Think about Nehemiah for a moment. He faced adversity on a massive scale. God called him to rebuild the walls of Jerusalem, a task that came with relentless opposition and discouragement. The threats were so bad that the Bible tells us the men worked with one hand and held a weapon in the other to defend themselves. Yet despite the challenges, Nehemiah chose to trust in God's plan and keep working. He didn't let bitterness or self-pity take root. Instead, he pressed on, and through that perseverance, he found joy in walking faithfully with God.

Trials do one of two things: they make us bitter, or they make us better. It's up to us to decide which one it will be. Jonah had the scorching winds and the withered plant to contend with. Nehemiah had opposition, exhaustion, and constant threats. One chose to grumble through adversity, while the other grew through it.

Choosing well isn't easy. It often comes when we're tired, irritated, or simply not in the mood to take the higher road. But I'll tell you something—the higher road leads to joy. It's the road that helps you sleep at night, the one that mends relationships and preserves peace. It's the road that reminds us of the blessings we have, even when life feels less than ideal.

We can either lean into God, using our trials as opportunities to grow through adversity, or we can choose to let adversity embitter us. There's something beautifully resilient, deeply faithful, and remarkably hopeful in the choice to be better, not bitter.

READ AND REFLECT

Read Jonah 4. What does Jonah's reaction to the plant reveal about where he placed his happiness?

Can you think of a time when your joy depended on something temporary—like your plans going smoothly or having things go your way? What difference do we see when our joy is rooted in God's unchanging character rather than in temporary comforts?

JOY IN GIVING

Use the space below to list three things you can do to bring someone else joy this week.

1. ____
   ____
2. ____
   ____
3. ____
   ____

LET'S MAP IT OUT

All the days of the oppressed
are wretched, but the
cheerful heart has
a continual feast.

Proverbs 15:15, NIV

Describes misery and suffering, whether due to external circumstances or internal struggles.

Refers to those burdened by troubles, hardships, or a negative outlook.

Symbolizes ongoing satisfaction, joy, and abundance, not tied to material wealth but to an attitude of the heart.

A joyful and contented spirit that remains positive despite circumstances.

While external trials may persist, our internal perspective — shaped by faith — has the power to bring lasting contentment and peace.

PRACTICALLY SPEAKING

Let's put this powerful principle into action. Over the next few days, try to identify one situation or event where you have a choice in how you respond. It could be a stressful situation at home, a challenging interaction with a co-worker, a personal setback, or even a global event that affects you.

Take a moment to pause and reflect before responding. Recognize the choice you have in that moment: will you let it make you bitter or better? If you feel yourself starting to react in a negative way, try to shift your perspective and choose the path of growth instead.

YOU'RE NOT IN THIS ALONE

Adopting a good attitude isn't always easy, but the good news is that we're not in this alone. It's a decision we make, yes—but it's not the whole story. The moment we take that first step toward forgiveness, healing, or simply letting go of bitterness, we're inviting the Holy Spirit to work within us. He equips us with the strength we need to move forward. Philippians 2:13 reminds us that "God works in you to will and to act in order to fulfill his good purpose." You don't have to muster up joy or patience on your own; the Holy Spirit produces that fruit in your life (Galatians 5:22-23). When bitterness knocks on your door, remember you're not alone. Ask God for help. He is faithful to give you the grace and strength to rise above the hurt, transforming your heart and renewing your mind as you lean on Him.

More Food for Thought...

A cheerful heart is good medicine, but a crushed spirit dries up the bones.
– Proverbs 17:22

Go, eat your food with gladness, and drink your wine with a joyful heart, for God has already approved what you do.
– Ecclesiastes 9:7

But may the righteous be glad and rejoice before God; may they be happy and joyful.
– Psalm 68:3

In all my prayers for all of you, I always pray with joy.
– Philippians 1:4

And we know that in all things God works for the good of those who love Him, who have been called according to His purpose.
– Romans 8:28

Thoughts and Jots

12

CREATE SPACE FOR GOD

I don't know about you, but I tend to get distracted easily. I can be working on something important, and the next thing I know, I'm scrolling through my phone or staring out the window at someone walking past the house. Distractions seem to pop up everywhere—the internet, phone notifications, random thoughts about dinner. Before I know it, the day has slipped away, and I'm left wondering where my time went.

Some nights, I find myself looking back at the day and asking, *Why didn't I use my time more wisely? Why do I keep getting pulled into these time-wasting traps?*

It's easy to get so caught up in the busyness of life that we miss out on the beauty and joy that surrounds us. We get too busy to notice the changing colors of the leaves or the way the sun filters through the trees. We rush from one task to the next, hardly pausing to take a breath—let alone to spend time with God.

> *For where your treasure is, there your heart will be also.*
>
> —Matthew. 6:21

We get so distracted by the search for joy that we don't realize it's already surrounding us. Joy isn't found in a perfect life, free from challenges. It's discovered in the quiet moments when we pause to recognize God's goodness in the midst of it all. It's that quiet assurance that, even when life feels overwhelming, His love remains constant. God's faithfulness gives us reason to smile, to take a breath, and to be grateful—even when the road is rough.

There's a reason Jesus told His disciples to "Come with me by yourselves to a quiet place and get some rest" (Mark 6:31, NIV). He knew the importance of slowing down, of stepping away from the noise and distractions to reconnect with the Father. But if we're honest, how often do we do that?

Many of us live life "flying by the seat of our pants," reacting to whatever comes our way instead of intentionally planning time for what truly matters. The expression comes from early pilots who, when their instruments failed, had to rely on their instincts to guide the plane—not exactly the safest way to fly. And it's not the best way to live, either.

If we want to live with purpose, we need to set our compass. That means deciding what's truly important and making sure our lives reflect those priorities. If we only pray when we feel like it, we miss out on the times we need it most. If we only read the Bible when it's convenient, we're likely to push it aside when life gets busy.

The truth is, we need to create space for God in our lives—not as an afterthought, but as a priority. It might mean saying no to certain distractions or carving out time each morning to sit quietly with the Lord. It might mean looking up from our phones to appreciate the beauty of His creation or pausing to thank Him for the simple joys in life.

When we set our compass toward Him, we find the peace and joy we've been too busy to notice. Because where our treasure is, there our heart will be also (Matthew 6:21). Let's make sure our hearts are aligned with the One who brings true joy.

Come with me by yourselves to a quiet place and get some rest. —Mark 6:31

READ AND REFLECT

Read Ecclesiastes 3:1-11. Take a moment to write your own Ecclesiastes 3 list. What are some things you need to make time for in your life? For example, 'a time to spend in God's Word,' 'a time to rest,' or 'a time to connect with loved ones.' Use this exercise to refocus your priorities and recognize what truly matters.

TODAY I'M THANKFUL FOR

Use the space below to list three things that you're thankful for.

1. ______________________________

2. ______________________________

3. ______________________________

3 WAYS TO CULTIVATE JOY

1. CELEBRATE GOD'S CREATION: ADMIRE THE BEAUTY OF A SUNRISE, FLOWERS, OR EVEN THE STARS.
2. MEMORIZE SCRIPTURE: HIDE GOD'S WORD IN YOUR HEART TO DRAW ON IN MOMENTS OF DIFFICULTY.
3. SERVE OTHERS IN HIS NAME: JOY GROWS WHEN WE SERVE OTHERS SELFLESSLY.

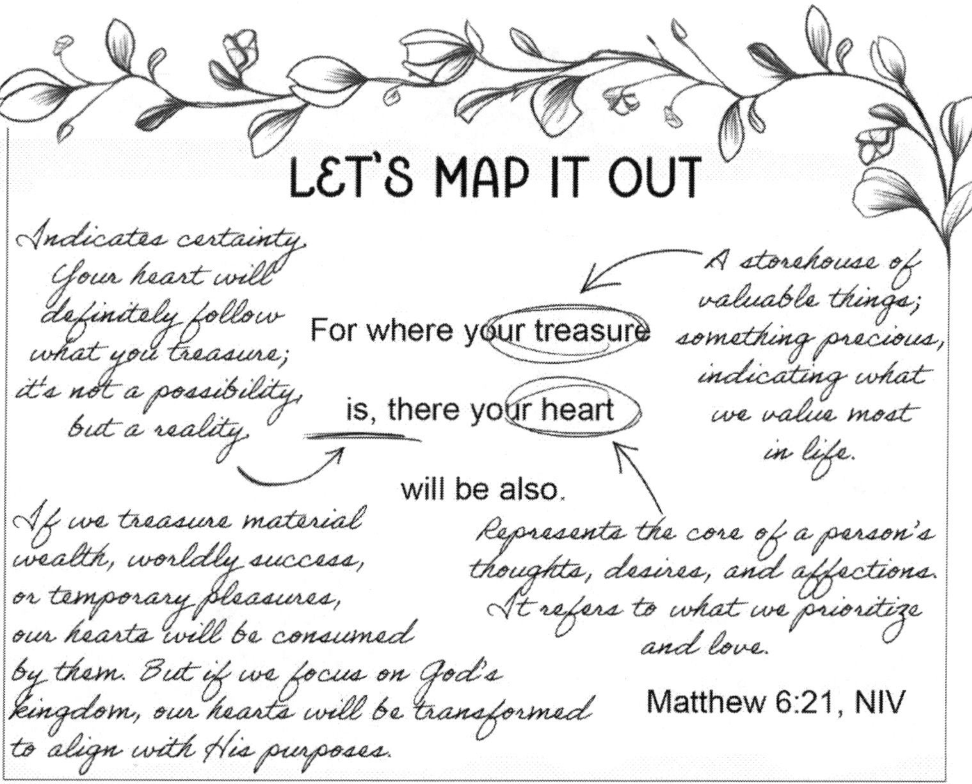

More Food for Thought...

But seek first his kingdom and his righteousness, and all these things will be given to you as well.
– Matthew 6:33

Take delight in the LORD, and he will give you the desires of your heart.
– Psalm 37:4

Come to me, all you who are weary and burdened, and I will give you rest.
– Matthew 11:28

Splendor and majesty are before Him; strength and joy are in His dwelling place.
–1 Chronicles 16:27

One thing I ask from the Lord, this only do I seek: that I may dwell in the house of the Lord all the days of my life, to gaze on the beauty of the Lord and to seek him in his temple.
–Psalm 27:4

Thoughts and Jots

13

DON'T GIVE WORRY THE KEYS TO YOUR JOY

> *Do not be anxious about anything, but in every situation, by prayer and petition, with thanksgiving, present your requests to God.*
>
> —Philippians 4:6

I used to think stress was just a normal part of life — a badge of responsibility we all carry. But as I've gotten older, I've come to realize that stress is often a cover for fear. When I say, "I'm stressed," what I'm really admitting is, "I'm afraid." Afraid things won't work out, afraid I won't measure up, afraid of what tomorrow might bring.

And let's be honest — stress is easy to justify. It can make us feel like we're being responsible, like we're doing what needs to be done. But if we peel back the layers, we'll find fear underneath. Fear of losing control. Fear of disappointment. Fear of embarrassment. Fear of the unknown.

I can't tell you how many times I've prayed, "Lord, I trust You," only to catch myself moments later running anxious scenarios in my mind. It's as if I'm saying, "I trust You… but let me hold on to this one thing, just in case." Sound familiar? If it does, you're not alone.

Like a thief in the night, fear quietly slips through the cracks of our minds, stealing the joy God has placed in our hearts. We tell ourselves we're just being cautious, bracing ourselves for the worst, but what we're really doing is giving worry the keys to our joy.

God never intended for us to carry that burden. To experience joy — true, unshakable joy — we must release our worries and place our trust in His care, knowing with confidence that we're safe in His hands. In Matthew 10:29, Jesus reminds us how much we're valued by God, saying, "Are not two sparrows sold for a penny? Yet not one of them will fall to the ground outside your Father's care." When we truly grasp that truth, joy begins to take root.

Some days that's easier said than done. Our minds love to race through every "what if," thinking we'll be prepared and protected. But here's the thing: those "what ifs" do nothing to change the future. They just rob us of joy in the present. The turning point comes when we decide to hand those fears over to God, trust that He's faithful, and pray.

Philippians 4:6-7 tells us, "Do not be anxious about anything, but in every situation, by prayer and petition, with thanksgiving, present your requests to God. And the peace of God, which transcends all understanding, will guard your hearts and your minds in Christ Jesus." But don't miss the connection: thanksgiving shifts our perspective from fear to joy. It reminds us of God's goodness and His faithfulness through every season of life.

It's in leaning on God that we experience joy—not because life is perfect, but because He is faithful.

READ AND REFLECT

Read 2 Chronicles 20:1-30. What did Jehoshaphat's men do as they marched toward the enemy, and what does their response teach us about trusting God during uncertain times?

LET'S MAP IT OUT

To be overly concerned, worried, or distracted by cares of life. It implies being pulled in different directions by worry

A broad term for communicating with God, emphasizing worship and devotion.

Do not be **anxious** about anything,

but in every situation, by **prayer**

and **petition**,

A specific request or plea for help, typically addressing a pressing need.

Grateful acknowledgment of God's grace and provision.

with **thanksgiving**,

present your requests to God.

To make known, to declare openly, to communicate clearly.

This verse reminds us that God is both willing and able to handle our concerns, offering us peace in return.

Philippians 4:6, NIV

WHAT WE CAN LEARN ABOUT WORRY FROM 2 CHRONICLES 20

2 Chronicles 20 offers us valuable lessons on handling worry. When faced with overwhelming fear, King Jehoshaphat chose to turn to God rather than give in to anxiety. Here are some key takeaways from this powerful chapter.

THE BATTLE BELONGS TO THE LORD

When several armies threatened Judah, Jehoshaphat could have panicked or taken matters into his own hands. Instead, he sought God's guidance. In return the message was clear: "Do not be afraid or discouraged because of this vast army. For the battle is not yours, but God's" (2 Chr. 20:15). This verse reminds us that we don't have to carry our burdens alone. We can release our worries to God trusting He will handle what we can't.

TAKE IT TO PRAYER

Rather than trying to solve the crisis himself, Jehoshaphat called the people of Judah to fast and pray. He openly admitted his fear and said, "We do not know what to do, but our eyes are on you" (2 Chr. 20:12). This shows us that we don't need all the answers. We simply need to bring our worries to God, trusting that He will guide us through.

RESPOND WITH WORSHIP

Jehoshaphat's response to God's promise was worship. Notice that they praised Him *before* seeing results. As they marched toward the enemy, they sang, and God led them to victory. Like Jehoshaphat, let's respond with worship *before* our trial is over, trusting that God is already at work.

TODAY I'M THANKFUL FOR

Use the space below to list four things that you're thankful for.

1. ______________________________

2. ______________________________

3. ______________________________

4. ______________________________

More Food for Thought...

The redeemed of the Lord will return and enter Zion with singing; everlasting joy will crown their heads. Gladness and joy will overtake them, and sorrow and sighing will flee away.
– Isaiah 51:11

Rejoice in the Lord and be glad, you righteous; sing, all you who are upright in heart!
– Psalm 32:11

You have filled my heart with greater joy than when their grain and new wine abound.
– Psalm 4:7

Be joyful in hope, patient in affliction, faithful in prayer.
– Romans 12:12

Though you have not seen Him, you love Him; and even though you do not see Him now, you believe in Him and are filled with an inexpressible and glorious joy.
–1 Peter 1:8

Thoughts
and Jots

14

THAT YOUR JOY MAY BE FULL

My brother in law Jerry is one of a kind. And when I say he's incredible, I'm not even close to describing how wonderful he is. He's the type of guy who would swim through shark-infested waters to get my sister a lemonade if she were thirsty. I don't know how he'd bring it back without spilling the glass, but you get the idea.

> *I have told you this so that my joy may be in you and that your joy may be complete.*
>
> —John 15:11

After he retired, Jerry packed a lunch each and every day, along with a pretty little tablecloth, and went downtown to meet Bonnie at work. He's the kind of guy who walks on the street side of the sidewalk—a little extra protection from oncoming traffic, not to mention the splashing water. He opens car doors, carries groceries, and buys his wife a gift on the 9th of every month to celebrate their kissing anniversary. After 41 years, that's a whole lot of gifts!

Perhaps the most adorable thing Jerry's ever done for Bonnie is stock up on chocolate. He understands how women work and knows that we can be

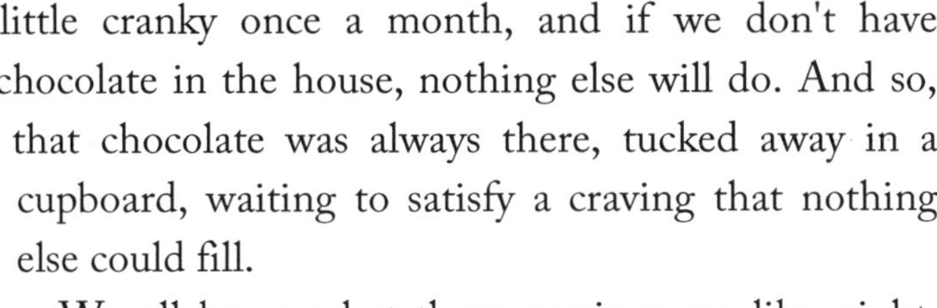

a little cranky once a month, and if we don't have chocolate in the house, nothing else will do. And so, that chocolate was always there, tucked away in a cupboard, waiting to satisfy a craving that nothing else could fill.

We all know what those cravings are like, right, ladies? We dig through the cupboards looking for chocolate—maybe for you it's something crispy and salty—and when you're looking for chocolate, nothing else will do.

As I got to thinking about that today, I was reminded of life. How we crave that certain something to make us happy—the perfect job, a bigger house, the person who will finally make us feel loved. Like a roller coaster, we chase high after high, but the high never lasts. Sure, those things might satisfy us for a season, but they'll never truly fill the space that can only be filled by God.

The truth is joy isn't something we can get from what we have or what we do. It's a gift from God. Jesus said in John 15:11, "I have told you this so that my joy may be in you and that your joy may be complete." That's the kind of joy we want—the kind that sticks around no matter what's going on in life, because it comes from knowing Jesus.

When we let Jesus fill our hearts with joy, we stop chasing things that leave us feeling empty. Instead, we feel at peace, knowing that we are loved by Him. His joy keeps us going when life is hard, and it gives us hope when things feel out of control.

So, the next time you're digging through the cupboards looking for something to satisfy, let it remind you to turn your heart to the only One who can truly fill it. True joy is found in Jesus, and the best part is that it's always there, waiting for you—just like Jerry's stash of chocolate—a gift that never runs out.

READ AND REFLECT

Read Psalm 16:5-11. List four reasons the Psalmist gives for his joy and gladness.

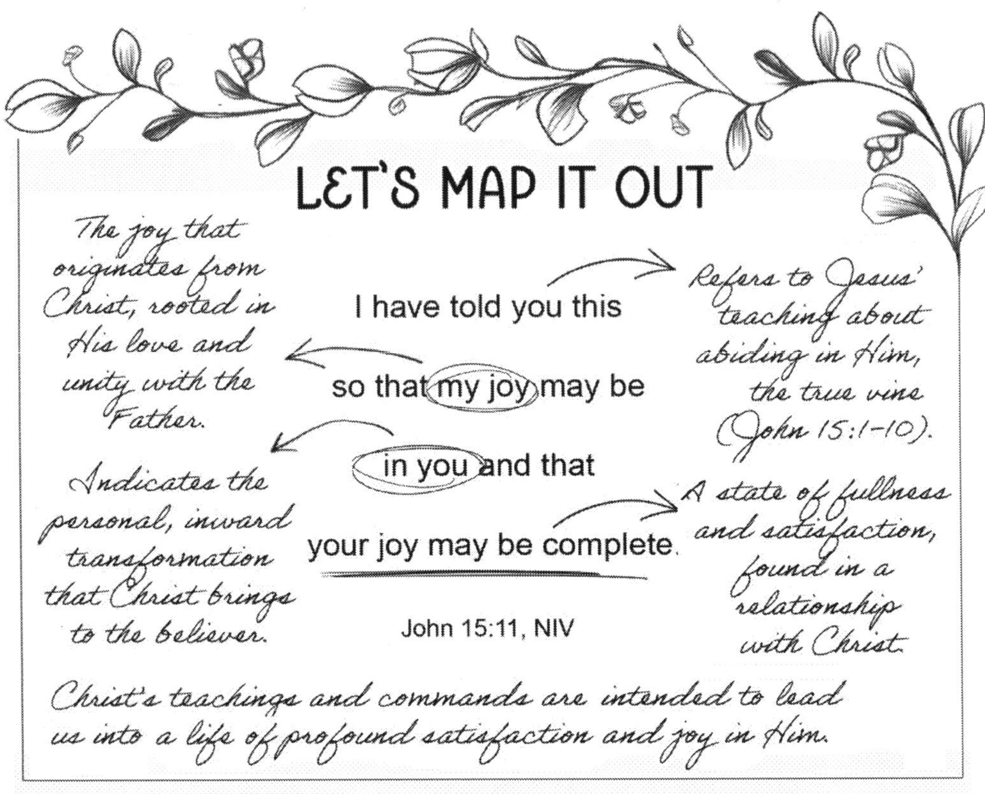

JOY IN THE SIMPLE THINGS

Use the space below to list four things that have brought you joy this past week:

1. ______________________________

2. ______________________________

3. ______________________________

4. ______________________________

CRAVING TRUE HAPPINESS

Charles Spurgeon once said, "We cannot be truly happy and live in sin. Holiness is the natural element of blessedness; and it can no more live out of that element than a fish could live in the fire. The happiness of man must come through his righteousness: his being right with God, with man, with himself — indeed, his being right all round."

Further on in the same sermon, he said: "His longing is not only to be treated as righteous by God, which comes through the atoning blood and righteousness of the Lord Jesus Christ; but that he may be actually righteous before the heart-searching God."

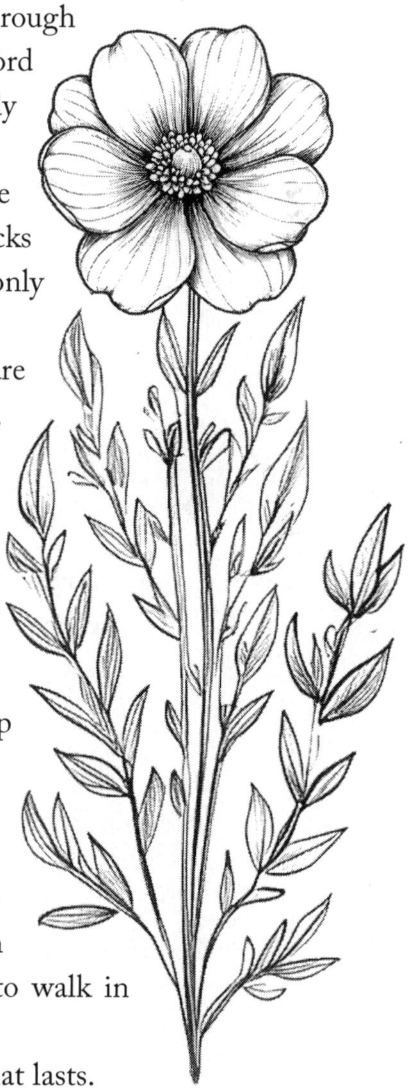

Think about that for a moment. We crave happiness, but true joy — the kind that sticks around no matter what life throws at us — is only found when we are right with God.

It's no surprise that Jesus told us: "Blessed are those who hunger and thirst for righteousness, for they will be filled." (Matthew 5:6)

The word "blessed" in Scripture speaks of a joy that goes beyond fleeting happiness. It describes a deep, lasting contentment that comes from knowing God and walking in His ways — the kind of joy that doesn't depend on circumstances, but on a relationship with Him.

The happiness we crave can't be found in temporary pleasures or worldly success. It's found in seeking God and His righteousness — not just being declared righteous through Christ's atoning blood, but actively longing to walk in righteousness before Him.

When we seek Him, He fills us with joy that lasts.

More Food for Thought...

I am coming to you now, but I say these things while I am still in the world, so that they may have the full measure of My joy within them.
– John 17:13

The Lord is my strength and my shield; my heart trusts in Him, and He helps me. My heart leaps for joy, and with my song I praise Him.
– Psalm 28:7

With joy you will draw water from the wells of salvation.
– Isaiah 12:3

Not that we lord it over your faith, but we work with you for your joy, because it is by faith you stand firm.
–2 Corinthians 1:24

The Lord has done great things for us, and we are filled with joy.
– Psalm 126:3

Thoughts and Jots

15

THE JOY OF AN INTENTIONAL LIFE

I'll be honest with you—back in the day, I was not one to keep things tidy. Growing up, my bedroom looked more like a battlefield than a peaceful retreat. Clothes? On the floor. Bed? Never made. Dresser? Covered in clutter. And you know what? I got used to it. I stepped over the mess every day, convincing myself it wasn't a big deal, until my parents finally forced me to clean up. And would stay clean for a few days, and then the cycle would start all over again.

Fast forward to now. Life looks a lot different with the kids grown and out of the house. And you know what I've discovered? Keeping things in order isn't all that hard when you do a little bit each day. It's actually refreshing to walk into a clean space—a home that feels peaceful and inviting. But let me tell you, that realization didn't just apply to my home; it reached into other areas of my life, too.

> *The thief comes only to steal and kill and destroy; I have come that they may have life and have it to the full.*
>
> —John 10:10

Because, here's the thing: procrastination doesn't just affect our cleaning habits. It has a sneaky way of creeping into our responsibilities, our relationships, and yes, even our faith. It whispers, "You've got time. Do it later." Later, I'll pay that bill. Later, I'll make that phone call. Later, I'll spend time in prayer. Later, I'll forgive. Later, I'll surrender to God.

But here's the truth: "Later" is a lie. It's a trap we fall into to ease our own guilt about putting things off. And the longer we delay, the heavier that burden becomes. It's like leaving your dishes pile up in the kitchen, day after day. Each time you walk in there, the pile grows a little bigger, and the weight of it—both physically and emotionally—starts to affect you. A chaotic life drains us. It robs us of peace, and that's exactly what the enemy wants. Jesus warned us in John 10:10, "The thief comes only to steal and kill and destroy; I have come that they may have life and have it to the full." Jesus is talking about false teachers here, but even so, worry can be one of those thieves. It may not rob us physically, but it steals our peace, drains our energy, and keeps us from living a life abounding in joy.

Look at that verse again. Notice that Jesus didn't say, "I've come so that *someday* you'll have an abundant life." No. He wants to give that life to us now. A life that goes far beyond merely surviving. A life that thrives spiritually and emotionally because of our connection to Christ.

It's found in the here and now—in the ordinary moments where we choose to live intentionally. It's in the joy of a tidy kitchen. The calm of a cleared-off table. The peace of a heart that's right with God.

Procrastination robs us of that joy. It convinces us that it's okay to keep putting off the things that matter. But here's the truth, my friend: God is calling us to move. To take action. Whether it's cleaning up a mess, mending a relationship, or spending time in His Word, there's freedom on the other side of obedience.

So, let's stop turning away from what needs to be done. Let's stop believing the lie that "later" is good enough. Today is the day to experience the fullness of life that Jesus promised. Not someday. Today.

Don't put off till tomorrow what you can do today. – Benjamin Franklin

LIFE IN ABUNDANCE

WHAT IT IS	WHAT IT ISN'T
Spiritual fulfillment	Material wealth or success
Freedom from sin & fear	A trouble-free life
Joy and peace in Christ	Waiting for heaven to experience joy
Purpose and hope	Perfect circumstances
Eternal life with God	Temporary happiness

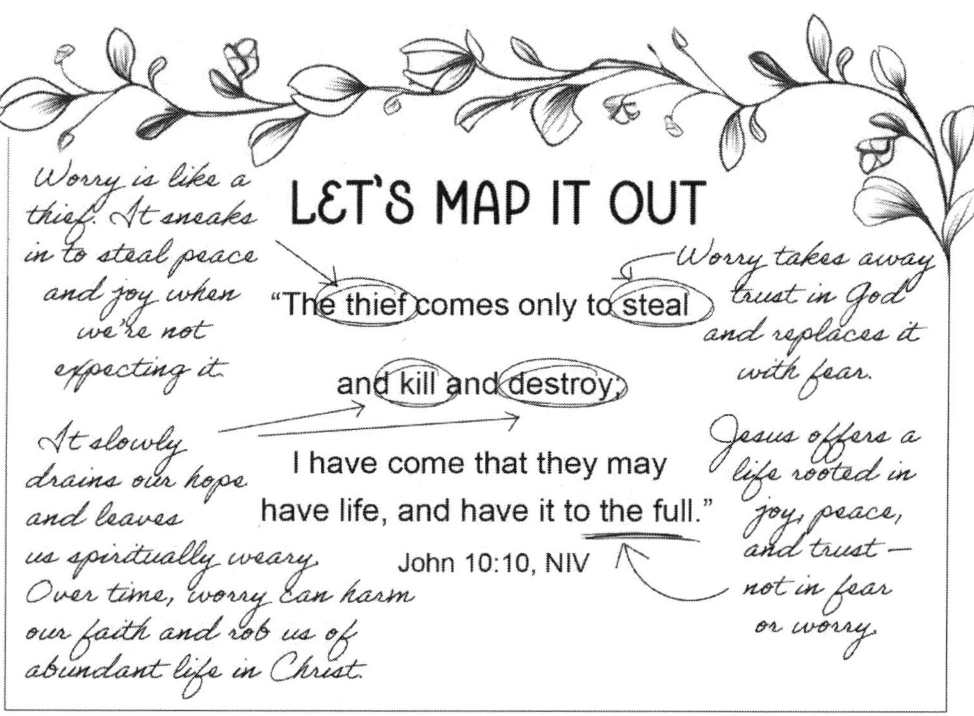

10 Practical Ways to Live Intentionally & Make Room for Joy

1. **TIDY UP IN 10 MINUTES**
   SET A TIMER FOR 10 MINUTES EACH DAY TO TACKLE CLUTTER. SMALL EFFORTS ADD UP OVER TIME, KEEPING YOUR HOME PEACEFUL AND ORDERLY. A TIDY SPACE OFTEN LEADS TO A CLEARER MIND AND HEART.

2. **HANDLE IT ONCE**
   IF A TASK TAKES LESS THAN FIVE MINUTES (LIKE PUTTING DISHES AWAY OR SENDING A QUICK MESSAGE), DO IT RIGHT AWAY. DON'T LET LITTLE THINGS PILE UP AND STEAL YOUR PEACE.

3. **MAKE THE BED**
   A SIMPLE TASK LIKE MAKING YOUR BED SETS A POSITIVE TONE FOR THE DAY. IT'S A SMALL WIN THAT CREATES A SENSE OF ORDER RIGHT FROM THE START — A REMINDER THAT EVEN LITTLE THINGS CAN BRING JOY.

4. **FORGIVE FIRST**
   JOY CAN'T FLOURISH WHEN WE'RE HOLDING ON TO GRUDGES. PRACTICE FORGIVING OTHERS — EVEN WHEN THEY DON'T ASK FOR IT. FORGIVENESS FREES YOUR HEART AND MAKES ROOM FOR PEACE AND JOY.

5. **LET GO OF RESENTMENT**
   HOLDING ON TO RESENTMENT WEIGHS US DOWN AND BLOCKS THE JOY GOD WANTS TO GIVE US. RELEASE IT THROUGH PRAYER, AND TRUST GOD TO HEAL WHAT'S BROKEN. "LET ALL BITTERNESS AND WRATH AND ANGER BE PUT AWAY FROM YOU" (EPHESIANS 4:31).

6. **SCHEDULE QUIET TIME WITH GOD**
   DON'T WAIT FOR THE PERFECT MOMENT TO SPEND TIME WITH GOD. EVEN 5-10 MINUTES EACH MORNING CAN BRING PEACE AND CLARITY TO YOUR DAY. IT'S IN HIS PRESENCE THAT WE FIND FULLNESS OF JOY.

7. **CHOOSE PROGRESS OVER PERFECTION**
   PERFECTIONISM CAN LEAD TO PROCRASTINATION AND OVERWHELM. INSTEAD, CELEBRATE SMALL WINS AND EMBRACE PROGRESS. JOY ISN'T FOUND IN DOING THINGS PERFECTLY — IT'S FOUND IN WALKING FAITHFULLY.

8. **PRACTICE COMPASSION**
   LOOK FOR WAYS TO SERVE OTHERS — EVEN IN SMALL WAYS. JOY GROWS WHEN WE TAKE THE FOCUS OFF OURSELVES AND SHOW KINDNESS TO THOSE AROUND US. COMPASSION SHIFTS YOUR HEART OUTWARD AND BRINGS LIGHT TO OTHERS.

9. **PRAY BEFORE YOU REACT**
   WHEN EMOTIONS RISE, PAUSE AND PRAY BEFORE REACTING. ASKING GOD FOR WISDOM AND GRACE IN THE MOMENT HELPS YOU RESPOND WITH KINDNESS AND MAKE ROOM FOR PEACE AND JOY.

10. **END THE DAY WITH GRATITUDE**
    BEFORE YOU GO TO BED, REFLECT ON THREE THINGS YOU'RE THANKFUL FOR. GRATITUDE SHIFTS YOUR MINDSET FROM OVERWHELM TO JOY AND REMINDS YOU OF GOD'S FAITHFULNESS — EVEN IN DIFFICULT SEASONS.

More Food for Thought...

Be very careful, then, how you live—not as unwise but as wise, making the most of every opportunity, because the days are evil.
– Ephesians 5:15-16

Whatever you do, work at it with all your heart, as working for the Lord, not for human masters, since you know that you will receive an inheritance from the Lord as a reward. It is the Lord Christ you are serving.
– Colossians 3:23-24

Teach us to number our days, that we may gain a heart of wisdom.
– Psalm 90:12

The wisdom of the prudent is to give thought to their ways, but the folly of fools is deception.
– Proverbs 14:8

She watches over the affairs of her household and does not eat the bread of idleness.
– Proverbs 31:27

Thoughts
and Jots

JOYFUL REFLECTIONS

CONVERSATIONS WITH GOD

JOYFUL REFLECTIONS

CONVERSATIONS WITH GOD

JOYFUL REFLECTIONS

CONVERSATIONS WITH GOD

JOYFUL REFLECTIONS

CONVERSATIONS WITH GOD

JOYFUL REFLECTIONS

CONVERSATIONS WITH GOD

JOYFUL REFLECTIONS

CONVERSATIONS WITH GOD

Made in the USA
Coppell, TX
18 February 2025

46055445R00081